Western Main Lines

NEWBURY TO WESTBURY

Vic Mitchell and Keith Smith
in association with
Kevin Robertson

MP Middleton Press

Cover picture: An eastbound freight passes over the junction for the Marlborough branch at Savernake Low Level. Sadly the date and locomotive details were not recorded. No trace of the junction or the station now remains. (Lens of Sutton)

Published May 2001

ISBN 1 901706 66 4

Design Deborah Esher
Typesetting Barbara Mitchell

Published by
Middleton Press
Easebourne Lane
Midhurst, West Sussex
GU29 9AZ
Tel: 01730 813169
Fax: 01730 812601

Printed & bound by Biddles Ltd,
Guildford and Kings Lynn

INDEX

ACKNOWLEDGEMENTS

We are very grateful for the help received from so many photographers. Our thanks also go to A.E.Bennett, W.R.Burton, G.Croughton, A.Dasi-Sutton, M.A.N.Johnston, M.King, N.Langridge, D.Trevor Rowe, Mr D. and Dr S.Salter, E.Youldon and, as always, our wives.

I. Railway Clearing House map of 1947.

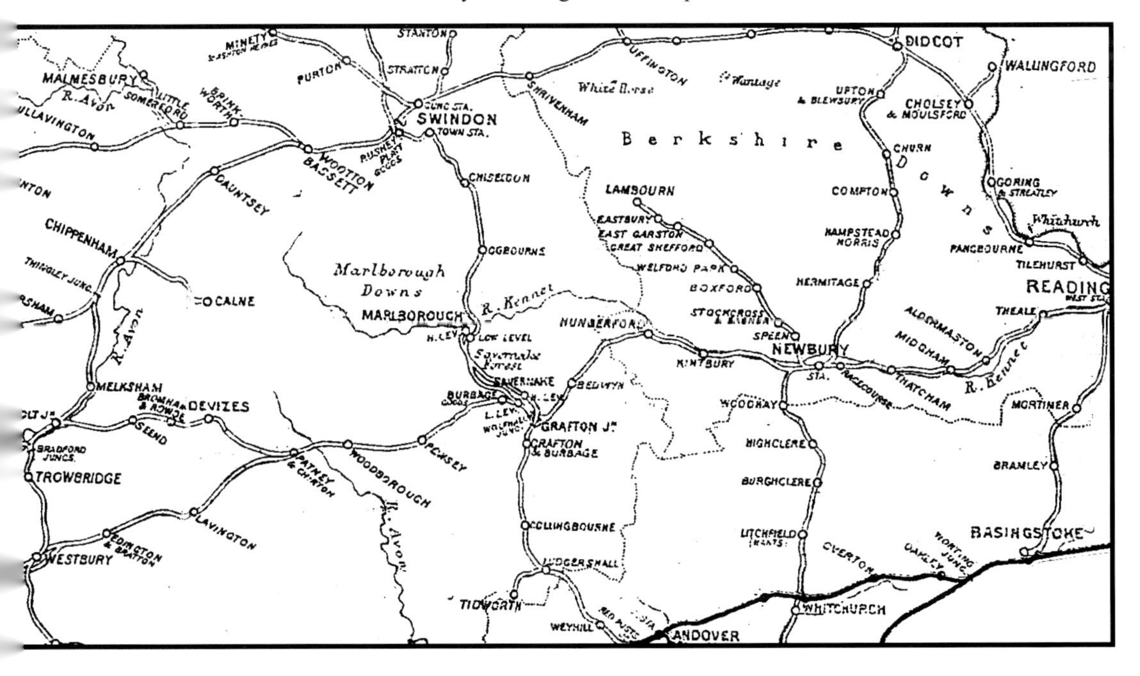

GEOGRAPHICAL SETTING

From Newbury to Hungerford the route climbs steadily up the Kennet Valley near to the Kennet & Avon Canal, which it remains close to, almost as far as Pewsey. The climb across a chalk subsoil continues from Hungerford to the summit at Savernake, from where a northward branch climbed close to Savernake Forest to reach the old market town of Marlborough.

The long descent to Westbury is through the Vale of Pewsey, mainly over Upper Greensand and Gault Clay. There are fine views of the Chalk escarpment of Salisbury Plain, which runs roughly parallel to the south side of the route for about 20 miles. The route crosses from Berkshire to Wiltshire between Hungerford and Bedwyn.

The Marlborough Branch began at Savernake on a small outcrop of Lower Greensand, but was predominantly on Chalk, much of it on the 500ft contour.

The maps are to the scale of 25 ins to 1 mile, unless shown otherwise.

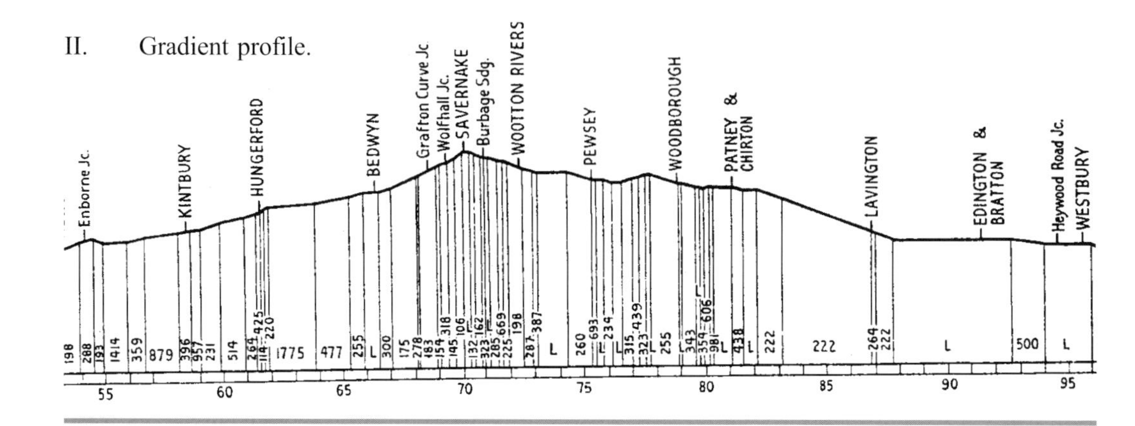

II. Gradient profile.

HISTORICAL BACKGROUND

The Berks & Hants Railway received its Act of Parliament in 1845 and services began between Reading and Hungerford on 21st December 1847, the line becoming part of the Great Western Railway.

Westbury received its first trains in 1848 from the north when the first part of the Wilts, Somerset & Weymouth Railway opened. It was extended to Frome in 1850 and it also became part of the GWR. A branch from this route to Devizes came into use in 1857.

The Berks & Hants Extension Railway received Royal Assent in 1859 and opened its line between Hungerford and Devizes on 11th November 1862. A branch from this to Marlborough first carried traffic on 14th April 1864. All these lines were controlled by the GWR and were of broad gauge until 1874, when a third rail was added. All trains were of standard gauge after 1892.

As part of a scheme to reduce journey times between London and the West of England, a more direct line between Patney & Chirton and Westbury was opened in 1900; for goods on 29th July and for passengers on 1st October. Further time saving was achieved with the completion of the Westbury Avoiding Line on 1st January 1933.

The direct routes remain open, but Devizes, Marlborough and some intermediate stations were closed in the 1960s. Details are given in the captions.

Newbury had secondary routes as follows: to Didcot (1882-1962), to Winchester (1885-1960) and to Lambourn (1898-1960).

There were no major changes until the GWR was nationalised in 1948, to become the Western Region of British Railways, when the visible changes were few. Trains began to appear in sector liveries - InterCity and Network SouthEast - in the mid-1980s - these being followed in the mid-1990s by Thames Trains and Great Western Trains colours as a prelude to privatisation. The former franchise related to services west to Bedwyn only. Both companies operated from 1996.

Marlborough Branch

The important market town on the London-Bath road was avoided by the main lines because of the difficult terrain. Thus a branch had to suffice and the Marlborough Railway Act was passed on 22nd July 1861; this allowed it to be leased to the GWR.

The branch was broad gauge and opened on 14th April 1864. Conversion to standard gauge took place on 1st July 1874.

A scheme to link the Midland Railway with the London & South Western Railway was active at that time. The first part opened eventually on 27th July 1881, under the title of the Swindon, Marlborough & Andover Railway. It linked the first two places. The section to Andover opened on 1st May 1882 and the route became the main part of the Midland & South Western Junction Railway. However, their trains had to use the GWR branch between Marlborough and Savernake, which resulted in much friction. In due course an independent double track was opened between these places by the MSWJR.

The GWR station at Marlborough lost its passenger service on 6th May 1933, but its neighbour was open until 11th September 1961. Freight closures are given in the captions.

PASSENGER SERVICES

These notes refer to down trains operating on at least five days per week and exclude non-stop services.

The service to the terminus of the route at Hungerford in 1850 comprised four trains on weekdays and two on Sundays. The 1870 timetable showed the same frequency to Devizes or beyond. One extra weekday journey had been added by 1890.

The 1901 timetable had five trains to Devizes (two on Sundays) and four to Westbury (weekdays only). By 1920, there was a complex service on weekdays comprising five trains to Devizes and five direct to Westbury, three of which were railmotors starting from Patney & Chirton. On Sundays, there were two via Devizes and only one direct. Thirty years on and there was still a similar number of trains, but more of the local trains ran via Devizes.

The 1966 timetable showed eleven stopping trains between Reading and Bedwyn (two more terminated at Hungerford) with four between Newbury and Westbury. The latter were withdrawn in April, when most of the intermediate stations were closed. On Sundays there were four or five to Bedwyn only. There has for long been an early evening semi-fast business train from Paddington.

In recent years, the service to Bedwyn has been approximately hourly, but there have been no departures from there westwards.

Timetables for June 1869 and January 1901 can be found by pictures 3 and 4.

Marlborough Branch

Four or five return trips were operated during the 19th century life of the line. A slip coach from London was provided in the early years of the next century.

The service frequency increased to ten by 1913, a figure that was still shown in the 1929 timetable. However, the GWR added a supplementary bus service that year, comprising seven trips, but four train journeys were cut out in the following year.

Both the branch train and the bus were withdrawn in 1933, after which time Marlborough was served by services on the former MSWJR route, which are described in our *Cheltenham to Andover* album.

SAVERNAKE and MARLBOROUGH.

Miles	Week Days only.	mrn		mrn		aft		aft		aft			
	2 London (Pad.)..dep.	..	..	7 15	..	2 45	..	..	..	6 0	..	..	..
—	Savernake H .....dep.	8 25	....	9 45	....	4 33	....	5 12	....	7 40	....	....	....
5¼	Marlborough J ...arr.	8 40	..	10 0	..	4 45	..	5 27	..	7 55	..	..	..

Miles	Week Days only.	mrn	mrn		aft		aft		aft				
	Marlborough J ...dep.	7 30	9 5	..	4 0	..	4 50	..	7 10	..	..	..	..
5¼	Savernake H 2, 7 arr.	7 42	9 17	....	4 15	....	5 2	....	7 25	....	....	....	....
75¼	7 London (Pad.)..arr.	10 0	1050	..	6 55	..	..	..	1025	..	..	..	..

H Low Level; about 250 yards to High Level Station. J High Level; about 300 yards to Low Level Station.

Road Motor Cars dep. Savernake (Low Level) for Marlboro (G. W. R. office) on Week Days at 9 25, 9 36, and 10 48 mrn., 1 3, 2 32, 6 10, and 8 25 aft., Sundays 6 3 aft.; returning on Week Days at 7 46, 8 56, and 10 9 mrn., 12 29, 2 2, 5 47, 7 11, and 7 59 aft., Sundays at 5 34 aft. Calling at Marlboro' Station Approach 3 minutes before arriving and departing Marlboro (G. W. R. office).

April 1932

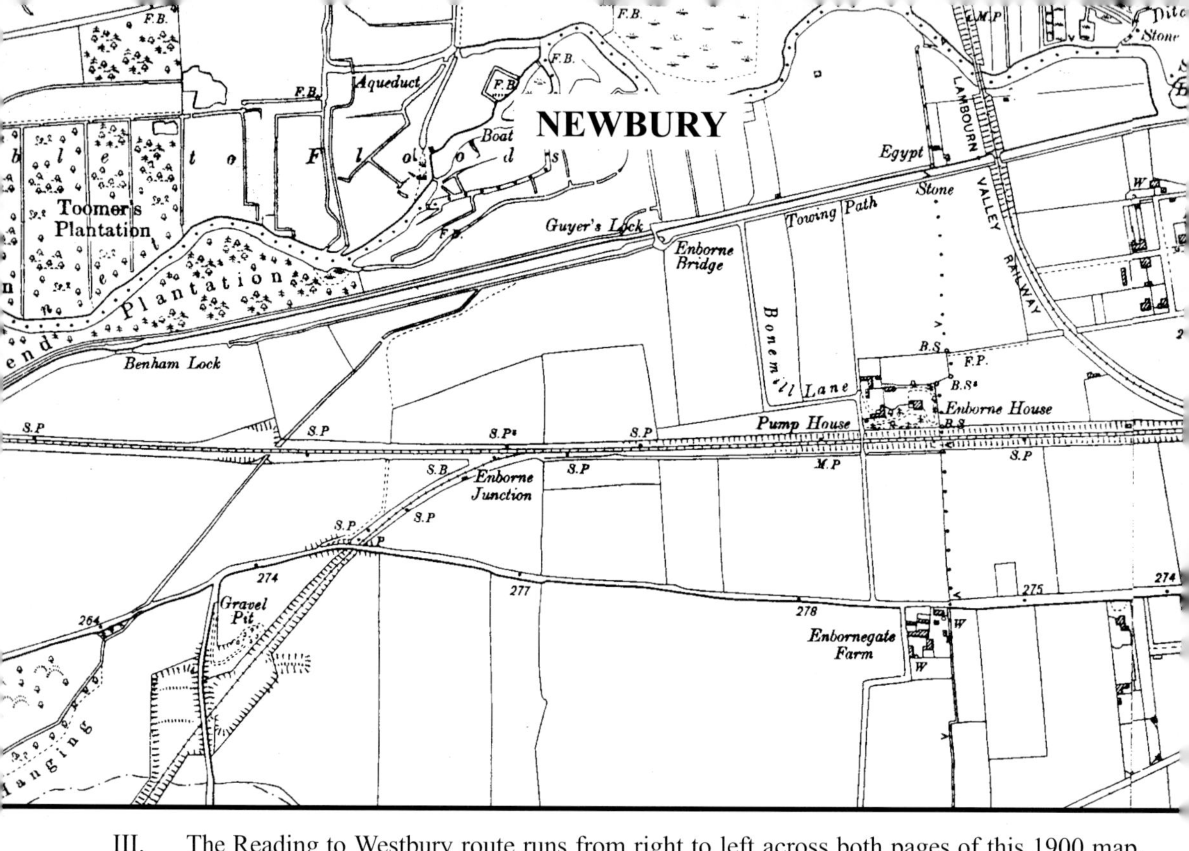

III. The Reading to Westbury route runs from right to left across both pages of this 1900 map, which is at the scale of 6 ins to 1 mile. Top right is the line from Didcot and lower left is the continuation of the route to Winchester. The Lambourn branch is shown on the left page; it had an independent third track from the station.

1. A westward view features the station after its rebuilding was completed in May 1910. Prior to that time, there were only two through lines and there was a roof spanning the tracks. The arm with holes in it is a backing signal. (Lens of Sutton)

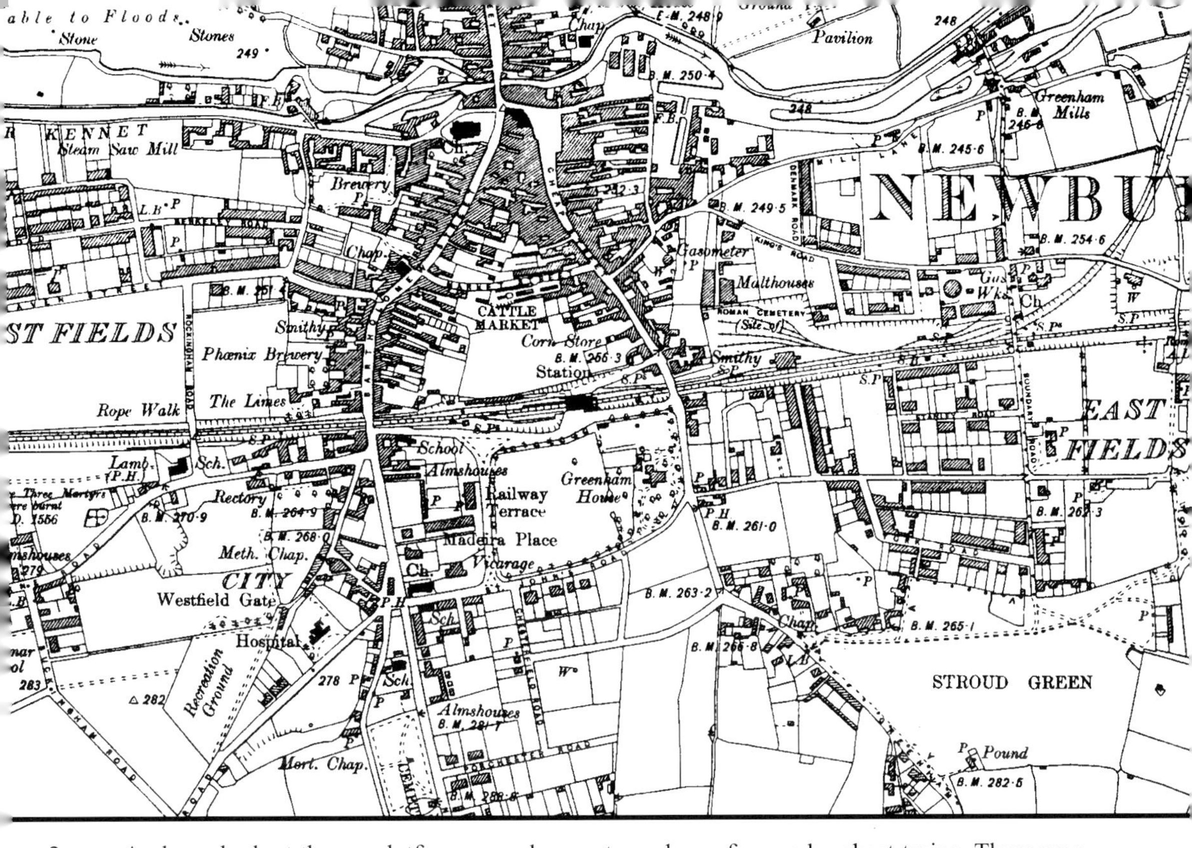

2. A closer look at the up platform reveals a water column for use by short trains. There was another behind the camera, at the end of the platform. On the right is the up bay, which is still used by local trains to London. The number of employees here rose from 50 in 1913 to 106 in 1936, but tickets issued fell from 159,000 to 131,000 over the period. (Lens of Sutton)

June 1869

READING, MARLBORO', DEVIZES, TROWBRIDGE, BRADFORD, BATH, BRISTOL, &c.—Gt. Westrn.

For Stas. to Reading, p. 8; from Basingstoke, p. 11; Richmond, &c. 40 & 39.

Down		Week Days						Sndys	
		1&2	1,2,3	1&2	1&2	1&2	1&2	1,2,3	1&2
LONDON :—		mrn	mrn	mrn	aft	aft	aft	mrn	aft
Paddington 8....dep		....	7 0	1010	2 0	3 30	5 10	9 0	4 45
Victoria 8 ...... ,,		....	6 28	8 30	1210	2 0	3 27	8 30	...
Kensington 8.... ,,		....	6 50	8 52	1232	2 23	3 49	8 52	....
Reading ....dep		....	8 45	1135	3 10	4 30	7 20	1040	6 15
Theale		....	8 57	1147	3 40	4 43	7 32	1052	6 28
Aldermaston		....	9 5	1154	3 55	4 52	7 40	11 0	6 36
Woolhampton		....	9 11	12 0	4 10	4 59	7 47	11 6	6 42
Thatcham		....	9 19	13 8	4 25	5 8	7 55	1113	6 50
Newbury 1		....	9 33	1220	4 40	5 21	8 5	1122	7 0
Kintbury		....	9 47	1233		5 35	8 20	1134	7 13
Hungerford		....	10 0	1247	Stop	5 47	8 35	1140	7 22
Bedwyn		....	1012	1 0	....	6 0	8 47	1155	7 37
Savernake		.. .	1022	1 10	....	6 8	8 55	12 5	7 47
Marlborough dep		....	10 0	1245	....	5 45	7 55	....	....
Marlborough arr		....	1040	2 0	....	6 30	9 15	....	....
Pewsey		....	1034	1 26	....	6 20	9 7	1218	8 0
Woodborough	1,2,3	....	1046	1 36	1&2	6 30	9 17	1227	8 10
Devizes .... arr	mrn	....	11 0	1 50	aft	6 45	9 30	1240	8 25
Devizes .... dep	7 10	9 10	11 5	1 55	3 50	7 0	Exp. Passengers leave Paddington at 6 20 aft.	1245	1, Station for Speen, Shaw, and Donnington.
Seend	7 20	9 20	1115	2 5	4 0	7 10		1255	
Holt Junction....	....	9 30	....	....	....	....		....	
Trowbridge 7 arr	7 40	5 40	1135	2 25	4 20	7 30		1 15	
SALISBURY 7 ar	9 20	....	1 30	4 5	....	9 20		8 40	
WEYMOUTH 7 ,,	1040	1 0	2 35	5 23	....	10 5		9 20	
Trowbridge ..dep	8 10	1&2 class	1155	3 5	4 30	8 5		1 20	
Bradford	8 22		12 5	3 20	4 40	8 15		1 30	
Freshford	8 28		1211	3 26	4 46	8 21		1 36	
Limpley Stoke ..	8 32		1215	3 30	4 50	8 25		1 40	
Bathampton 10 ..	8 42		1225	3 40	5 0	8 35		1 50	
Bath 9........arr	8 50		1230	3 45	5 20	8 40		2 0	
BRISTOL 9..arr	9 30	....	1 0	4 25	5 45	9 15		2 25	
EXETER 9.. ,,	1 25	....	4 30	9 15	9 15	2 50		6 50	
PLYMOUTH 14,,	4 18	....	6 30	1210	1210	5 10		9 50	

Up.		Week Days.							Sndys	
		1,2,3	1&2	1&2	1&2	1&2	1&2	1&2	1,2,3	1&2
		mrn	mrn	b	mrn	aft	mrn	aft	mrn	mrn
PLYMOUTH 10....dep		....	....	....	6 45	b 1,2,3 class locally, and also to Stations beyond Reading.	1025	1240	....	6 45
EXETER 10 ...... ,,		....	....	6 0	10 0		1225	3 15	....	9 45
10 BRISTL(TempleSt) ,,		6 40	....	1035	1 25		5 15	6 30	8 0	3 55
Bath ....dep		7 0	....	11 0	1 47		5 45	6 55	8 30	4 29
Bathampton		7 11	....	1111	1 57		5 56	7 8	8 35	4 38
Limpley Stoke		7 21	....	1119	2 7		6 6	7 20	8 45	4 48
Freshford............		7 25	....	1123	2 12		6 10	7 24	8 49	4 52
Bradford..............		7 32	...	1130	2 20		6 17	7 30	8 55	5 0
Trowbridge 7......arr		7 45	....	1140	2 30		6 27	7 40	9 5	5 10
WEYMOUTH 7....dep		6 0	....	9 0	1240		5 0	....		1030
SALISBRY(Fishrtn) 7,,		6 40	....	1015	1 40		....	6 40	Stop	8 5
Trowbridge........dep		8 5	10 0	1220	3 12		7 8	8 7	....	5 15
Holt Junction		8 10	1025	1230	3 20		....	8 15	....	5 25
Seend		....	1035	1240	3 30		....	8 25	1,2,3	5 35
Devizes .... arr		8 27	1050	1250	3 40		7 40	8 35	mrn	5 50
Devizes .... dep		8 30	1&2 exp.	1 5	3 45		7 45	....	8 20	5 55
Woodborough		8 42		1 18	3 57		7 51	....	8 23	6 10
Pewsey		8 50		1 28	4 7		8 5	....	8 42	6 20
Marlborough.. dep		8 40		1245	4 0		7 55	...	....	....
Marlborough.. arr		9 25		2 0	4 40		9 15	....	....	....
Savernake		9 0		1 44	4 18		8 15	....	8 55	6 33
Bedwyn		9 8		1 54	4 28		....	....	9 5	6 43
Hungerford	1&2	9 22		2 13	4 42		8 32	....	9 20	7 0
Kintbury	mrn	9 28		2 22	4 48		....	....	9 27	7 7
Newbury 1	7 40	9 37		2 39	4 57	6 25	8 50	....	9 40	7 20
Thatcham	7 48	....		2 47	5 5	6 35	....	....	9 48	7 30
Woolhampton....	7 54	....		2 55	....	6 50	....	....	9 55	7 38
Aldermaston	8 0	9 52		3 2	5 15	7 5	....	....	10 1	7 44
Theale .... {39, 5	8 12	10 0		3 16	5 23	7 25	....	....	1010	7 53
Reading 11, 8, 67, a	8 23	1012		3 30	5 35	7 50	9 15	....	1025	8 10
KENSINGTN 11 ar	1019	1239		5 35	7 48	9 43	....	....	3 24	....
VICTORIA 11 ,,	1035	1258		5 57	8 7	10 2	....	....	3 43	....
PADDINGTN 11 ,,	9 40	1115		4 45	6 50	9 40	1015	....	3 25	1010

3. No. 8430 takes water at the down platform on 2nd September 1953, while working a local service. The adjacent bay platform was often used for starting trains bound for Winchester, Southampton or the Hungerford route. (D.B.Clayton)

4. Bearing shedplate 82D (Westbury), 4300 class 2-6-0 no. 5385 departs west with the 4.36pm all-stations Newbury to Devizes on 7th July 1956. On the left is the Lambourn bay and West Box, which had 55 levers. The carriages on the right are standing at the horse dock. (R.C.Riley)

READING, NEWBURY, MARLBORO', WESTBURY, DEVIZES, TROWBRIDGE, &c.—Gt. Western.

Miles	Fares from Paddington 1 cl.	2 cl.	gov	Down.	Week Days mrn	mrn	mrn	mrn	mrn	mrn	non	aft	aft	aft	aft	aft	aft	aft	aft	aft	Sundays mrn	mrn	aft
				Paddington Station, London 2 ....dep.			6 30	9 5	Thursdays only.	9 55	12 0	1215	1 50	4 0		5 15	5 45			7 15	h	9 20	4 5
—	s. d.	s. d.	s. d.	Reading ....dep.			7 55	1015		1125	1257	1 47	3 5	4 55	5 30	6 10	6 34		6 50	8 15		1035	6 3[illegible]
5¼				Theale			8 9	1027		1139		2 2	3 19	5 11	5 43				7 2	8 29		1047	6 42
8¾	7 6	4 9	3 9	Aldermaston			8 18	1035		1148		2 10	3 27	5 19	5 52				7 10	8 37		1055	[illegible]
10¾				Midgham			8 25	1041		1156		2 16	3 33	5 25	5 59				7 16	8 44		11 2	6 57
13¾				Thatcham			8 34	1048		12 4		2 23	3 40	5 32	6 7				7 23	8 52		1110	[illegible]
17	8 10	5 6	4 5	Newbury 23, 22			8 46	1059		1217	1 21	2 34	3 52	5 43	6 15	6 38	6 58		7 34	9 5		1121	7 18
22¼				Kintbury			8 57	1110		1228		2 45	4 3	5 54					7 45	9 16		1132	7 28
25½	10 3	6 6	5 1½	Hungerford			9 6	1116	1118	1237	Stop	2 51	4 13	6 3		6 53	Stop		7 51	9 27		1141	7 38
30¼				Bedwyn			9 16		1128	1247			4 24	6 14						9 37		1151	7 48
34				Savernake 76			9 27	Stop	1138	1258			4 37	6 25		7 10			Stop	9 47		12 1	7 58
39½	12 6	8 0	6 3½	Marlboro' arr.			9 48		1152	1 21			5 15	6 42		7 27							
				Marlboro' dep.			9 3		1115	1237			4 17	6 0		6 52							
39¼				Pewsey			9 38		1148	1 9			4 48	6 36		7 21				9 57		1212	8 9
42¾				Woodborough			9 47		1156	1 18			4 58	6 47		7 30		7 45		10 5		1222	8 19
—	13 6	8 6	6 9	Patney and Chirton			9 53		12 2	1 24			5 4	6 55				7 51		1011		1228	8 25
—				Patny & Chirton d			10 0			1 30			5 15					7 55					
—	14 6	9 0	7 3	Lavington			1019			1 49			5 34					8 14					
—	15 3	9 6	7 7½	Edington & Bratton			1027			1 57			5 42					8 22					
—	16 0	10 0	7 11½	Westbury 20, 22 a			1036	mrn		2 6	aft		5 51				aft	8 31					
50	14 8	9 0	7 1½	Devizes	6 30	8 30	10 6	11 0	1210	1 35	2 25		5 16	7 8		7 46	7 57			1022	8 35	1240	8 36
54½				Seend	6 38	8 38	1014	11 8		1 43	2 33		5 24				8 7		aft	1030	8 43	1251	8 44
58				Holt 21	6 46	8 46	1022	1116		1 51	2 42		5 32				8 15		9 29	1039	8 51	1259	8 52
61	16 0	10 0	7 11½	Trowbridge 20, 22 arr.	6 54	8 52	1028	1124		1 57	2 49		5 38			8 4			8 34	1044	8 57	1 5	8 58
89½	16 0	10 0	8 0	Salisbury 22 arr.	8 35	1030	1218	1b55		4 45	4 45		7b15						11 0			8 50	
124	23 10	15 0	11 11	Weymouth 20 "	9 53	1220	1 10	2 30		4 17	6 20		8 35					11 0	11 0	9h10	1150	1010	
73½				Bath * 22 "	8 3		1110	12 5		3 5	4 26		6 42						9 32		10 5	2 5	
85				Bristol 2 "	8 38		1135	1233		3 30	4 48		7 5						9 56		1040	2 30	

Miles from Trowbridge	Up.	mrn	mrn	mrn	mrn	mrn	mrn	mrn	mrn	aft	mrn	aft	aft	aft	aft	aft	aft	aft	aft	aft	Sundays mrn	aft
												Thursdays only.	Thursdays only.									
	Temple Meads, Bristol 10 ....dep.		6 5				8 12	10 0	1140		1123	c				2 15			5c30	6 42		3 45
	Bath * 22 .... "		6 23				8 36	1021	1156		1143					2 37			5 50	7 9		4 15
	Weymouth 21. "				6 40		6 40	8 10			1015				1 35	1 35	4 20		4 20	5 20		1035
	22 Salisbry (Fshrtn) "		5 50					1059			1035				2 40	1 5	4 40		4 40	7 35		8 10
	Trowbridge ......dep	6 45	7 15				9 35	1143			1238					3 40			6 43	8 58	5 55	5 25
3	Holt	6 55					9 45	1152								3 50			6 52	9 7	6 2	5 34
7	Seend	7 5					9 53	12 0			1253					3 58			7 0	9 15	6 11	5 43
11½	Devizes	7 21	7 39				10 9	1210	1238		1 8		2 30			4 16			7 17	9 25	6 26	6 0
—	Westbury ....dep.				9 14						1235				3 48		6 30			Stop		
—	Edington & Bratton				9 21						1245				3 58		6 40					
—	Lavington				9 32						1253				4 6		6 48					
—	Patny & Chirton ar				9 50						1 11				4 24		7 6					
—	Patney and Chirton	7 31					1018				1 17		2 39			4 27	7 8		7 26		6 37	6 9
18½	Woodborough	7 40					1026				1 25		2 46			4 35	7 13		7 34		6 46	6 16
21½	Pewsey	7 47	7 59	8 13			1035				1 34		2 54			4 44			7 43		6 58	6 26
27½	Marlboro' arr.	Stop	8 35				11 5		1 21		2 15		3 20			5 15			8 15			
	Marlboro' dep.		7 52	7 52			1025		1237		1 30		2 35			4 17			7 37			
27	Savernake 76		8 11	8 30			1047		1 5		1 48		3 5			4 56			7 56		7 10	6 38
30½	Bedwyn			8 39			1056				1 57		3 13			5 4			8 5	aft	7 20	6 49
35½	Hungerford		8 27	8 53			11 8				2 9		3 22	3 30		5 16			8 18	9 42	7 31	7 1
38½	Kintbury	mrn		9 0			1115				2 16			3 37		5 23			8 26	9 48	7 38	7 8
44	Newbury 25, 22	7 53	8 42	9 15		1029	1130		1 37	1 55	2 30	3 10		3g48		5 37		7 30	8 40	10 0	7 52	7 26
47½	Thatcham	8 2		9 25			1140				2 39	3 19		4 19		5 46		7 39	8 49	10 7	8 1	7 34
50½	Midgham	8 8	8 53	9 33			1148				2 45	3 25		4 25		5 52		7 45	8 55	1012	8 8	7 41
52½	Aldermaston	8 14		9 40			1155				2 51	3 31		4 31		5 59		7 51	9 1		8 15	7 49
55½	Theale ...... [183, 115	8 24		9 50			12 6				3 0	3 39		4 39		6 8		7 59	9 8	a	8 25	7 59
61	Reading 10, 2, 36, arr.	8 34	9 9	10 1		1054	1219			2 26	3 11	3 50		4 50		6 19		8 10	9 20	1030	8 35	8 10
97	10 London (Pad.) arr.	9 45	1010	1055		1145	1 40		2 47	3 57	4 26	5 10		5 50		7 35		9 10	11 5	1145	1020	9 15

h Tuesday, Thursday, and Saturday mornings.

* Manvers Street; about ¼ mile from Queen Square Station (Midland).

a Calls at 10 18 aft. on Wednesdays. b L. & S. W. Station. c Stapleton Road. g Departs at 4 10 aft.

January 1901

5. Stopping trains were provided with a variety of motive power. No. 4962 *Ragley Hall* is about to depart with the 11.48am Westbury to Paddington on 5th March 1960. It ran via Devizes and stopped at all stations to Reading, with a twelve minute rest at Newbury. (R.C.Riley)

7. After seventeen miles of almost continuous downhill running from Savernake summit, no. 50024 rushes through with the 05.05 Penzance to Paddington "Golden Hind" on the crisp early morning of 24th April 1975. The cutting here had been widened greatly in 1909; this and other improvements were paid for mainly by the Didcot, Newbury & Southampton Railway. (G.Gillham)

←

6. The south elevation was photographed in about 1970. It had changed little in the previous 60 years and remained little altered in the subsequent 30. However, the staffing levels had dropped to single figures. Much of the space is now rented out for non-railway business. (British Rail)

8. A view of the west end of the station on 4th March 1978 shows two class 119 DMUs passing on services to and from Bedwyn. As from the following day this section of line was closed completely for two weeks to allow track rationalisation and the installation of colour light signalling, controlled from Reading Panel. West Box (left) closed on 16th April, Middle Box (obscured by the footbridge) on 4th March and East Junction on 20th March. (G.Gillham)

→

9. Painted in executive livery, an up HST speeds over the 1978 trailing crossover on 9th June 1984. The new larger radius curves took the track away from the platform edge. (P.G.Barnes)

This station is also featured in our *Didcot to Winchester* and *Slough to Newbury* albums.

→

10. A Gloucester Cross Country DMU heads west on 10th August 1984. These second generation units were superseded by Thames Turbos, which were introduced in 1992. The first generation was introduced by the GWR in 1934. (M.Turvey)

253030
L578

ENBORNE JUNCTION

11. The junction is shown on the left of the Newbury map. To assist with wartime traffic, an up goods loop was added from the junction (its signal box is in the mist) almost to the point of convergence of the Lambourn branch. Seen nearing completion, it came into use on 13th July 1943. Spring points protected the entry onto the up main line. (NRM)

12. An up goods train was diverted into the loop on 25th August 1944, but failed to stop before the signal and was derailed by the catch points shown in the previous picture. (NRM)

13. The signals for trains from Winchester are on the right as no. 2950 *Taplow Court* passes with the 2.35pm Paddington to Bristol on 21st July 1951. The 39-lever signal box was closed and the goods loop taken out of use on 29th January 1967. The line south had shut on 10th August 1964. The A34 Newbury Bypass now passes over the route, just behind the camera. (NRM)

EAST OF KINTBURY

14. No. 7788 is approaching Hamstead Crossing from the east with a typical local train on 21st June 1957. The crossing is a little over two miles from Kintbury and carries an unclassified road to Marsh Benham. (E.W.Fry)

15. Traffic did not warrant a block post here until 1907. This box dates from March 1921 and was photographed in October 1977. Lifting barriers and CCTV were installed prior to its closure on 17th April 1978. The barriers were still operated from Kintbury in 2001. (K.Robertson)

16. The signal box was probably secondhand when it arrived here and was fitted with a nine-lever frame. Two more levers on a separate wicket frame were added later for gate locks. (K.Robertson)

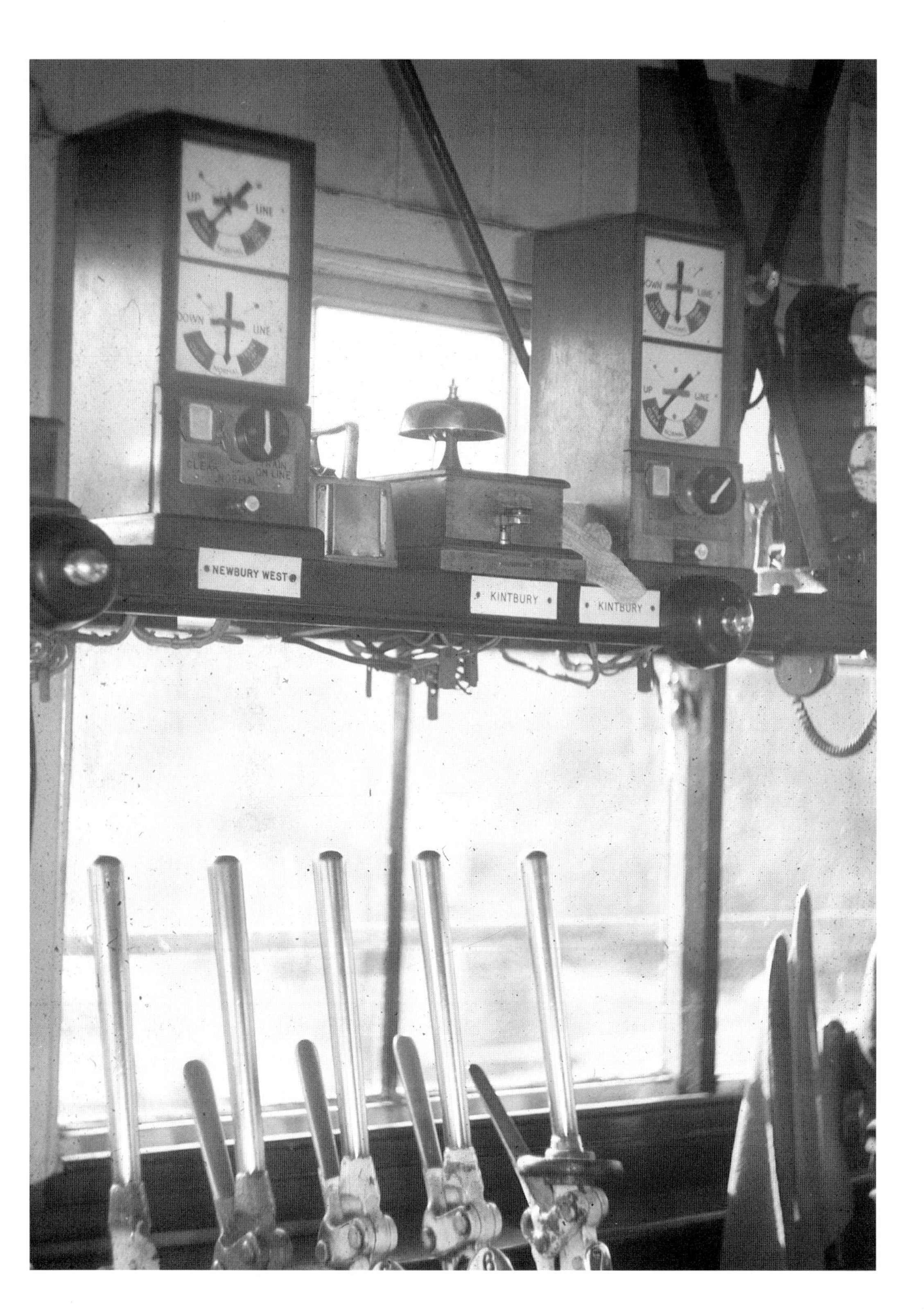
UP LINE
DOWN LINE
CLEAR
NEWBURY WEST
KINTBURY
KINTBURY
UP LINE

KINTBURY

17. An eastward view includes a tall co-acting signal halfway along the down platform, and some of the staff. There were nine or ten men employed between the wars. We are probably viewing one shift, minus the signalman. (Lens of Sutton)

IV. The 1936 survey reveals the close proximity of the station (right) to both the canal and the river.

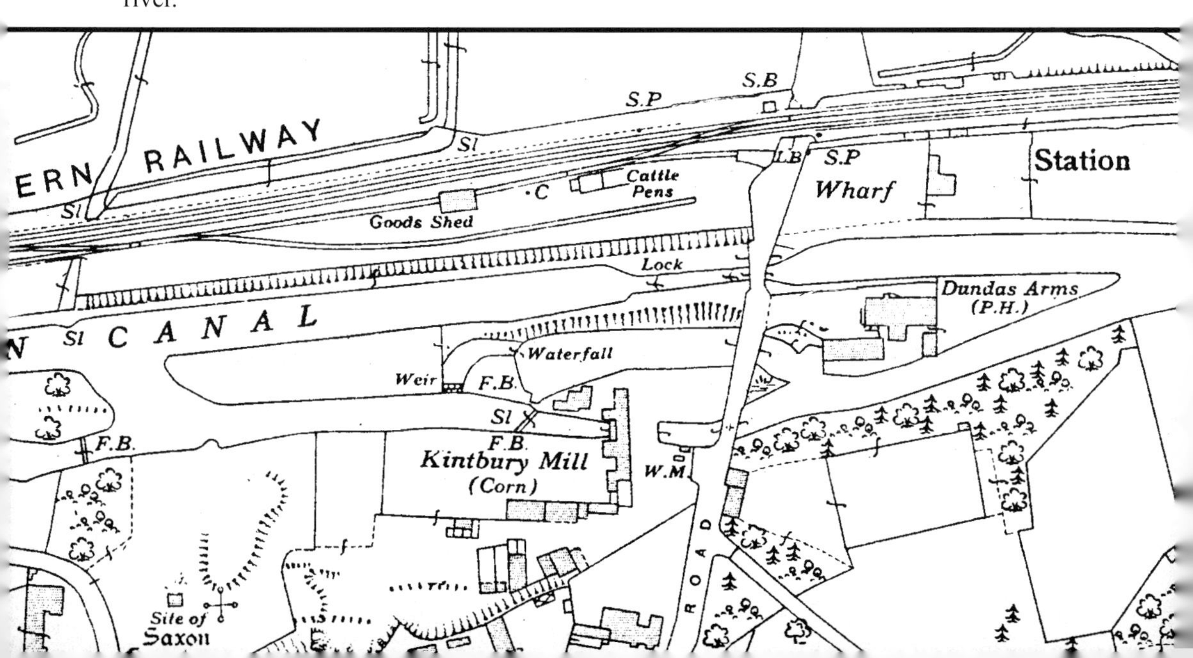

18. The station is situated on the northern edge of the village and the road in the background links it with the A4, so numbered in 1919. The track gang made an unusual subject for a postcard. (Lens of Sutton)

19. A 1919 photograph shows the revised position of the down signal and also the up platform extension. The ground signal is for the trailing connection into the goods yard. (LGRP/NRM)

KINTBURY

1B53

20. Staffing ceased on 2nd November 1964 and most of the buildings were demolished soon after. It was officially "Kintbury Halt" from that time until 5th May 1969. The local population was still under 2000. (Lens of Sutton)

22. A Bedwyn-Reading DMU arrives on 29th May 1976, as an express speeds west. The crossing gates had been replaced by full lifting barriers on 4th October 1974. (C.L.Caddy)

21. Class 52 no. D1021 *Western Cavalier* heads the 12.26 Saturdays-only Paddington to Penzance on 8th September 1973. It is passing the site of the goods yard which closed on 19th May 1964, but continued to receive coal until 7th September of that year. The end-loading dock is still evident. (G.Gillham)

Kintbury	1903	1913	1923	1933
Passenger tickets issued	23659	22870	23629	23313
Season tickets issued	*	52	137	92
Parcels forwarded	15356	31443	25402	15841
General goods forwarded (tons)	2920	2476	2515	926
Coal and coke received (tons)	1867	1913	1959	549
Other minerals received (tons)	370	851	2797	7752
General goods received (tons)	2075	3072	1622	759
Trucks of livestock handled	65	51	71	18

(* not available. Seasons include holiday Runabouts.)

23. Photographed on the same day, the 1947 20-lever signal box lasted until 17th April 1978. The CCTV monitors and controls for the barriers on the adjacent level crossings were moved from it to the larger hut shown in the next photograph. (C.L.Caddy)

24. The well lit station is in the background as a class 47 runs west on 9th June 1984. The rear coach is near the gate box. The view is from a bridge which crosses the canal and railway. (P.G.Barnes)

HUNGERFORD

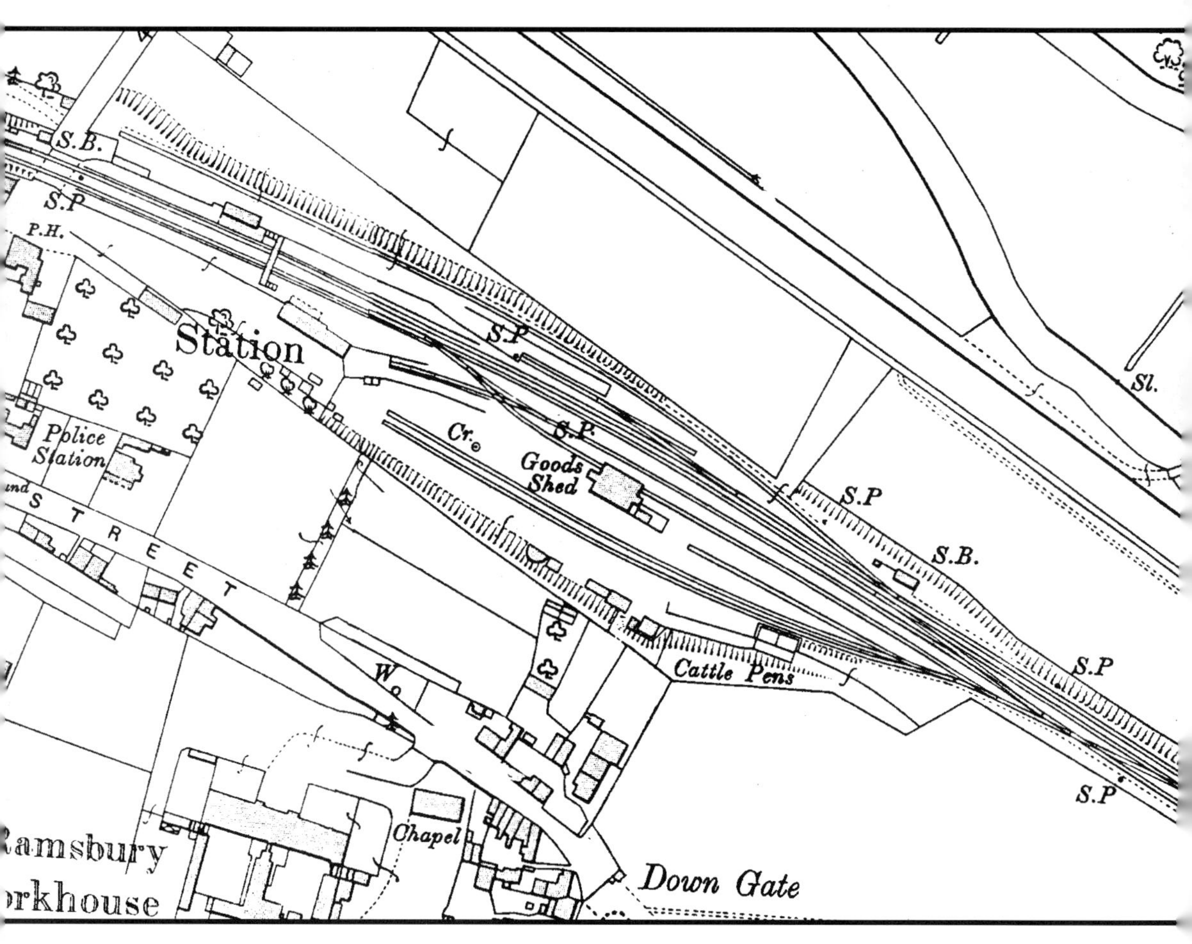

V. The 1909 survey shows the main building parallel to the boundary fences and not the track. This suggests that it dates from the era of the terminus, prior to 1862. New curved platforms were provided in about 1900, together with a footbridge. There was a turntable here as late as 1876.

Hungerford	1903	1913	1923	1933
Passenger tickets issued	37238	36261	36456	38673
Season tickets issued	*	79	173	220
Parcels forwarded	35292	46676	48520	63754
General goods forwarded (tons)	7521	6031	5112	1818
Coal and coke received (tons)	1692	794	995	800
Other minerals received (tons)	996	2810	4006	6741
General goods received (tons)	8072	8188	6483	4244
Trucks of livestock handled	260	565	325	150

(* not available. Seasons include holiday Runabouts.)

25. An up train runs past the signal box and over the level crossing, prior to stopping for the gathered crowd. Note the locomotive inspection pit in the foreground. The route westward was doubled in 1898. (Lens of Sutton)

26. Steam railmotors were introduced on some GWR local services in about 1905. The engine was on one bogie; a cylinder cover can be seen below the left buffer. No. 74 was in use from 1906 to 1933. Such vehicles were soon working both routes west from Patney & Chirton. (Lens of Sutton)

GENTLEMEN
WATERLOO

27. A 1919 panorama shows equine transport to still be unchallenged by motors here. There was no road access to the up side. Lighting was by gas, although the lanterns differed. There was a staff of about 15 at this time. (LGRP/NRM)

Great Western Railway.
MARLBOROUGH TO
NEWBURY
.THIRD CLASS
Issued subject to the conditions stated on the Co's. Time Bills. (HL)
Newbury Newbury
544

28. There were two signal boxes until 19th January 1939, this one being doubled in size in the previous year in readiness for its extra duties. Both had 39-lever frames. It is seen in 1946, but was demolished by a derailed freight train on 10th November 1971. The nameplate had been painted black during the war. (K.Robertson coll.)

29. Seen from the footbridge on 6th July 1959 is 2-6-0 no. 6302 with the 11.20am Bristol to Reading, which ran via Devizes. The 6-ton crane and the cattle pen are visible in the goods yard, which remained in use until 1st July 1970. Staffing ceased on 2nd November 1964; the term "Hungerford Halt" was applied from that time until 5th May 1969. (R.M.Casserley)

31. A train of 27 stone wagons derailed in the early hours of 10th April 1971, damaging the up platform and leaving only the lever frame of the signal box in place. Both lines were blocked, but single line working was established later. Another stone derailment occurred on 5th September 1994, near the up goods loop. The result is seen two days later as no. 166210 passes, while working the 11.24 from Bedwyn to Paddington. Introduced as Network Turbos, the class 165/1 was built at York in 1992-93. (S.P.McMullin)

30. Approaching with down milk empties on 8th July 1956 is no. 6965 *Thirlestaine Hall*. It is running alongside the down goods loop, which came into use on 11th April 1943. The canal is obscured by the hedge on the left. (R.C.Riley)

32. Signalled for the down goods loop on 19th May 1977 is no. 47157 with an empty stone train running from Theale to Westbury. The signals and the points were worked by electric motors owing to their great distance from the signal box. This view is from the bridge seen in picture 34. (G.Gillham)

166210

47 157

33. The 08.38 from Penzance was hauled by no. 50050 on 30th May 1978 and it passes the 38-lever replacement signal box, which lasted only until 17th July of that year. The road is little used, as it is a cul-de-sac. (G.Gillham)

34. A Bedwyn service approaches on 9th June 1984 having just passed the remnant of the down goods loop, which had become a siding in 1978. An up goods loop was laid further east, this coming into use in March 1980. (P.G.Barnes)

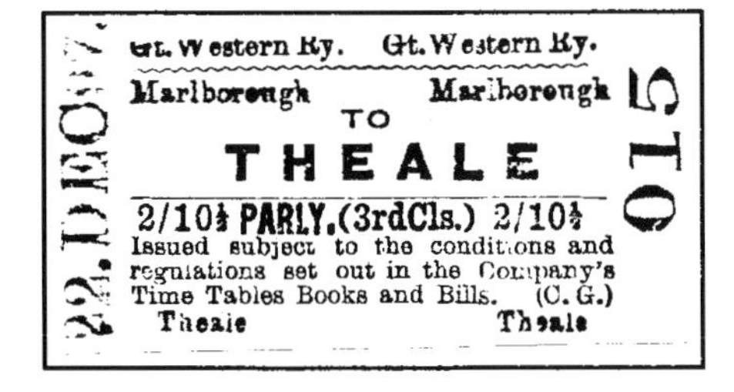

35. The platforms were rebuilt and new shelters provided in 1991. The original footbridge was retained, together with two roof supports for the lighting. Nos. 59002 and 59003 head a stone train from Merehead to Acton on 30th April 1997. The latter locomotive was destined for Germany via Wembley and Lille. (M.J.Stretton)

HUNGERFORD
L 410

EAST OF BEDWYN

36. There are ten locks between Hungerford and Bedwyn; this is the eighth and it is at Little Bedwyn. Passing on 2nd May 1994 is a Hertfordshire Railtour hauled by nos. 20131 and 20118. The English Electric Type 1s were seldom seen on the route and were normally used on freight work. There had been a signal box here until 1899 (named Little Bedwyn) and one at Fairfield Crossing from 1907 to 1951; it had a seven-lever frame. (M.J.Stretton)

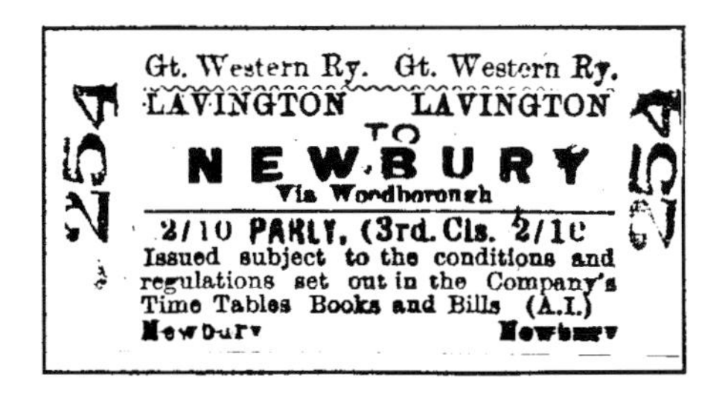

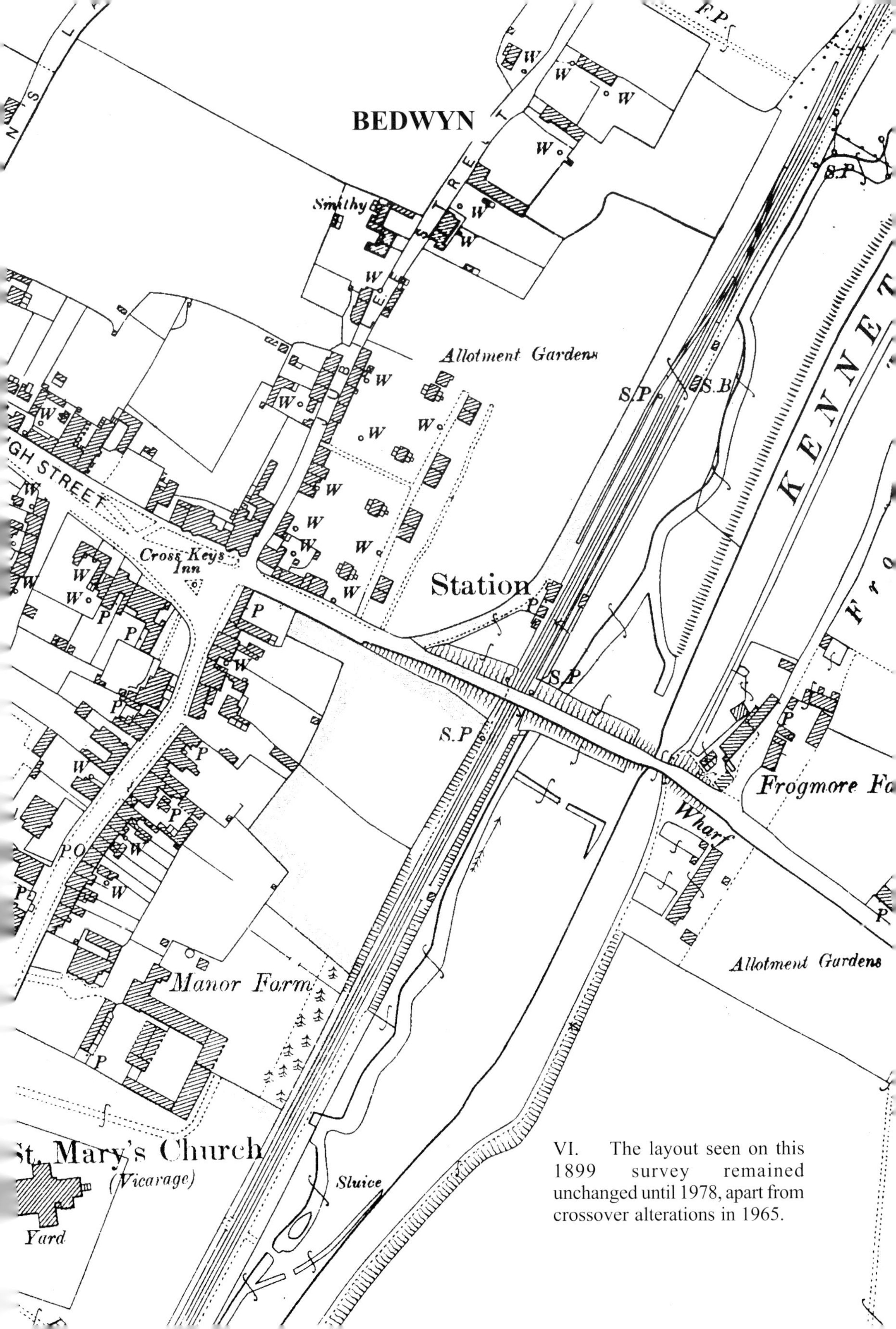

VI. The layout seen on this 1899 survey remained unchanged until 1978, apart from crossover alterations in 1965.

37. This 1919 eastward view includes the jib of the 3-ton crane, the well ventilated urinal and the 17-lever signal box, which was in use from 1897 to 11th September 1978. The route westward was doubled in January 1899. (LGRP/NRM)

38. The GWR had been pioneers in the field of road transport, both for goods and passengers. This 4-ton Thorneycroft was photographed in March 1928, at which time there was a staff of ten. The GWR's general manager, Sir Felix Pole, lived nearby. The 6.0pm from Paddington made its second stop here at 7.26, "upon request to the Guard". (K.Robertson coll.)

39. A view north in 1959 features the goods shed, the enlarged down side shelter and part of Great Bedwyn, which had a population of only 849 in the 1961 census. Goods traffic ceased on 7th September 1964. (R.M.Casserley)

219
G.W.R.
BEDWYN
219
GREAT
SPEED 12 M.P.H.
BEDWYN

BEDWYN

40. The approach to the up side and the goods yard was recorded in July 1959, at which time eight down trains called on Mondays to Fridays. The 1963-64 timetable showed four calling and five terminating trains. (H.C.Casserley)

41. The four flights of stairs to the road are shown in this February 1966 picture, but not on the map. By this period, the weekday down service comprised fourteen trains, ten of which terminated. Note that the bay had a white edge as it was used by DMUs ending their journeys here. (C.L.Caddy)

Bedwyn	1903	1913	1923	1933
Passenger tickets issued	11711	11463	12285	8745
Season tickets issued	*	*	64	78
Parcels forwarded	16092	17718	25485	57715
General goods forwarded (tons)	2456	1836	1518	1117
Coal and coke received (tons)	178	144	596	220
Other minerals received (tons)	80	417	174	2033
General goods received (tons)	1299	1399	904	1057
Trucks of livestock handled	23	14	24	72

(* not available. Seasons include holiday Runabouts.)

42. Local DMUs terminated in a new siding west of the road bridge from 11th September 1978, the points and crossover being controlled from Reading. A class 47 runs west with an extra train on 10th January 1987 and is seen from a DMU on layover. (P.G.Barnes)

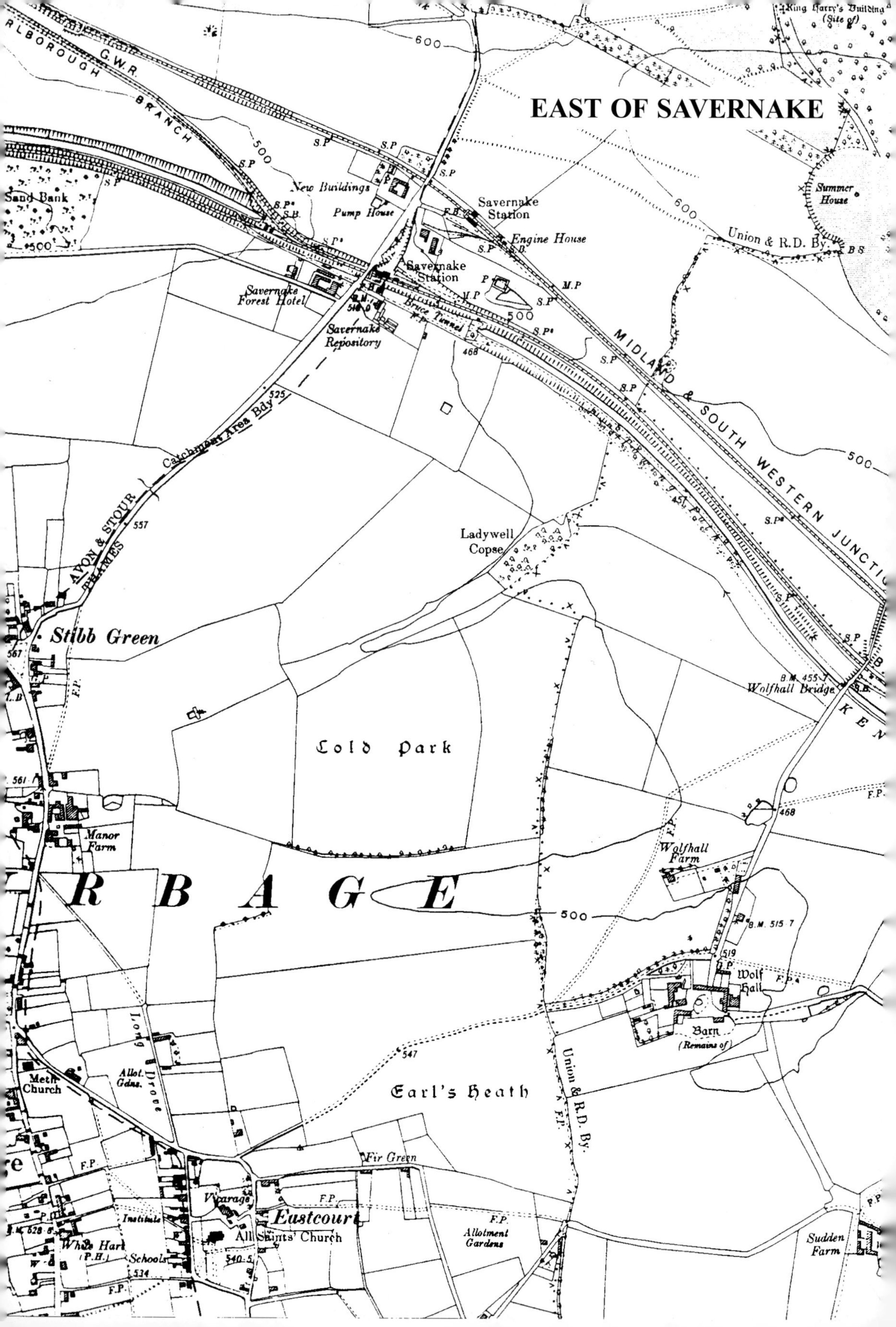
EAST OF SAVERNAKE
King Harry's Building (Site of)
G.W.R.
RLBOROUGH BRANCH
Sand Bank
New Buildings
Pump House
Savernake Station
Engine House
Savernake Forest Hotel
Savernake Repository
Bruce Tunnel
Summer House
Union & R.D. By.
MIDLAND & SOUTH WESTERN JUNCTIO
Catchment Area Bdy
AVON & STOUR
THAMES
Ladywell Copse
Stibb Green
Wolfhall Bridge
Cold Park
Manor Farm
Wolfhall Farm
RBAGE
Wolf Hall
Barn (Remains of)
Long Drove
Allot. Gdns.
Meth Church
Earl's Heath
Union & R.D. By.
Fir Green
Vicarage
Eastcourt
All Saints' Church
Institute
White Hart (P.H.)
Schools
Allotment Gardens
Sudden Farm

VII. The 1926 map at 6 ins to 1 mile has our route from Bedwyn on the right, together with a signal box, which was in use until 1967 and was simply a ground frame controlling a little-used level crossing. The Kennet & Avon Canal embraces the railway closely and penetrates GWR property at Savernake (left) by passing under the station in a tunnel. Through barge traffic between Reading and Bristol began in 1810, but railway competition later resulted in decline and the undertaking was purchased by the GWR in 1857. The MSWJR is so annotated, although it had been absorbed by the GWR in 1923. The lines to Marlborough are top left and the one to Andover is at the bottom.

Other views of these junctions and of both Savernake stations can be found in our *Cheltenham to Andover* album.

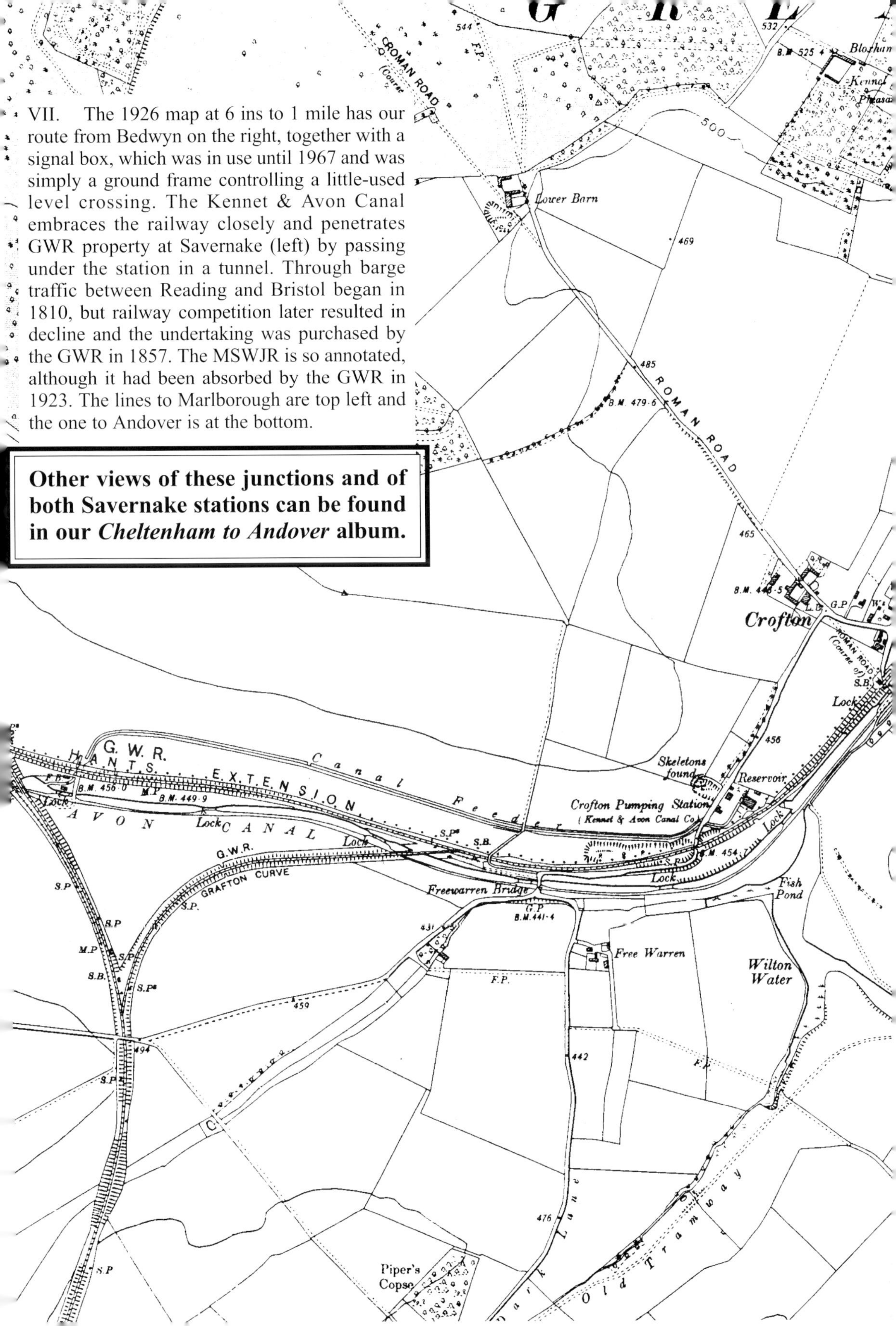

43. Crofton Pumping Station is to the right of the map and its purpose is to raise water from the nearby spring-fed Wilton Water and to send it along the "Canal Feeder" to supply the summit pound of the canal. Although photographed in 1958, we include the building, as it was GWR property for 91 years. Electricity took over that year. (H.C.Casserley)

←

44. The two beam engines reach almost to the top of the three-storey building and receive steam from two Lancashire boilers of the type seen here. The Kennnet & Avon Canal Trust purchased the site in 1967 and both engines and boilers were brought back to working order over the subsequent 20 years. The monsters can be seen in action on selected days: telephone 01672 870300 for details. (R.M.Casserley)

45. Grafton East Junction is shown on the centre of the left page of map VII and is seen from the east, as the 11.30am Torquay to Paddington approaches. The rusty line to Andover on the left only carried special trains, mainly military ones. It was known as Grafton Curve, as was the signal box from 1933. Its 17 lever frame, was functional from 6th September 1905 until 22nd September 1964, but the curve was taken out of use on 5th May 1957. (NRM)

46. Moving west, but looking east, we see the bridge which carried the 1898 MSWJR route over the GWR. It is marked on the left of the right page of map VII. Trains from Andover to Savernake Low Level used the second line from the right. The one on the right was a loop line and was in use until December 1958. (I.Peters)

47. A little further west (and just onto the left page of map VII), we come to Wolfhall Junction. The Andover lines and the loop are visible above the roof of Wolfhall Junction signal box, which had 26 levers and closed on 22nd November 1964. The route south was not used after 11th September 1961. (I.Peters)

SAVERNAKE

48. The station initially had one platform on a single line. A passing loop and bay platform were added when the Marlborough branch opened in 1864, but a platform was not provided for the loop until 1882. The bay is in the distance in this postcard view. (Lens of Sutton)

50. Another eastward view, but this is at the divergence of the lines. The Marlborough branch is above the mouth of the 502 yard long Bruce Tunnel, which runs diagonally under the station. Also included is a "Syphon" milk van and Savernake West box. (K.Robertson coll.)

←

49. Looking in the other direction in 1919, we witness a train in one of the two short parallel goods sidings. Wagons can also be seen in the down goods loop, which was provided with a cattle dock. A total of 15 men were employed in 1923, Burbage Goods Depot staff being included in this figure. (LGRP/NRM)

Savernake (Low Level)	1903	1913	1923	1933
Passenger tickets issued	18031	19544	16662	8016
Season tickets issued	*	*	63	18
Parcels forwarded	12262	14839	14241	42462
General goods forwarded (tons)	32	140	424	24
Coal and coke received (tons)	14	91	75	37
Other minerals received (tons)	13	66	461	80
General goods received (tons)	89	327	314	420
Trucks of livestock handled	3	69	12	74

(* not available. Seasons include holiday Runabouts.)

51. The first part of the branch was double track, this allowing the branch engine to run round its train after each journey. The gradient was too severe for the use of railmotors. Slip coaches for Marlborough were dropped by three passing down expresses by 1911 and then attached to the branch train, seen here in 1919. (LGRP/NRM)

52. The term "Low Level" was applied from 1st July 1924 to 11th September 1961. No. 5975 *Winslow Hall* is working a westbound freight on 6th July 1959 and is passing under the lane which leads to the High Level station, which is largely obscured by the trees on the left. (H.C.Casserley)

VIII. The diagram shows the arrangement existing in 1954. From 6th May 1933, the double track that was opened in 1898 became two parallel single tracks, the branch trains using the western one. The newer route was much less steeply graded, but had a 648 yard long tunnel through the chalk downs.

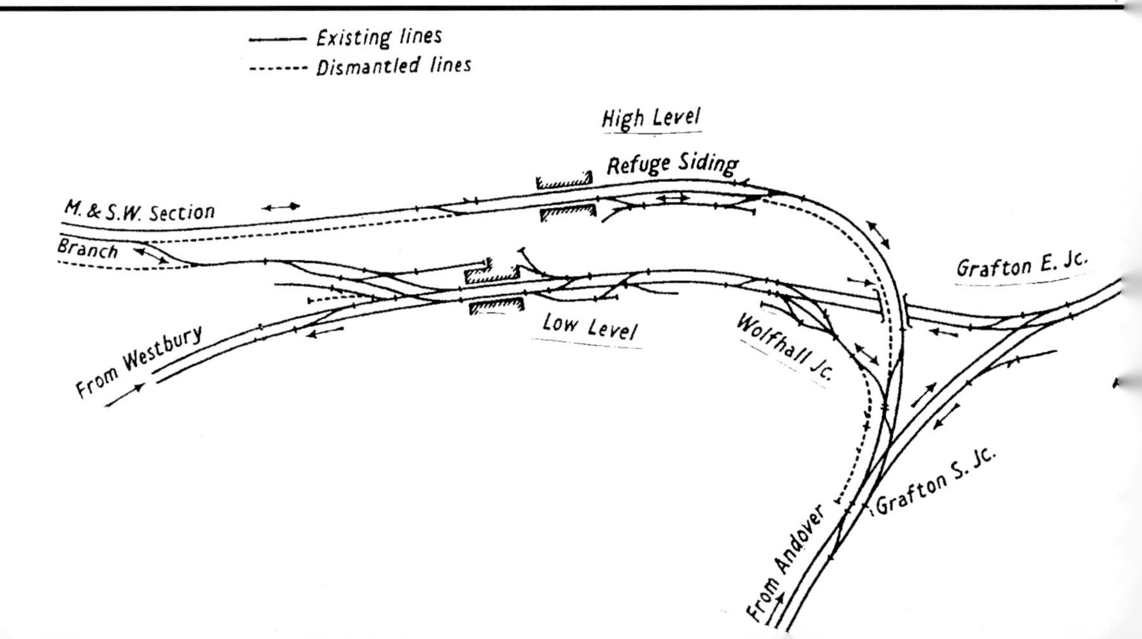

53. The entrance was from the lane just mentioned and is seen in 1959. Passengers changing to the High Level had to be fairly fit. However, all the Cheltenham to Andover trains began to use Low Level that year, owing to a chalk fall blocking the High Level line. (H.C.Cassserley)

54. No. D603 approaches with the up "Cornish Riviera" on 3rd June 1961, while U class no. 31808 waits with the 2.50pm Andover Junction to Swindon. Local goods traffic ceased on 19th May 1964 and the station closed to passengers on 18th April 1966. (E.Wilmshurst)

55. A class 50 heads an up train on 6th January 1979 and passes the derelict West Box, which was in use from January 1883 until September 1978, although rarely switched in during its final years. The route westwards had been doubled in 1899. East Box was at the east end of the goods loop until closed on 4th February 1968. East had 23 levers and West had 32. (P.G.Barnes)

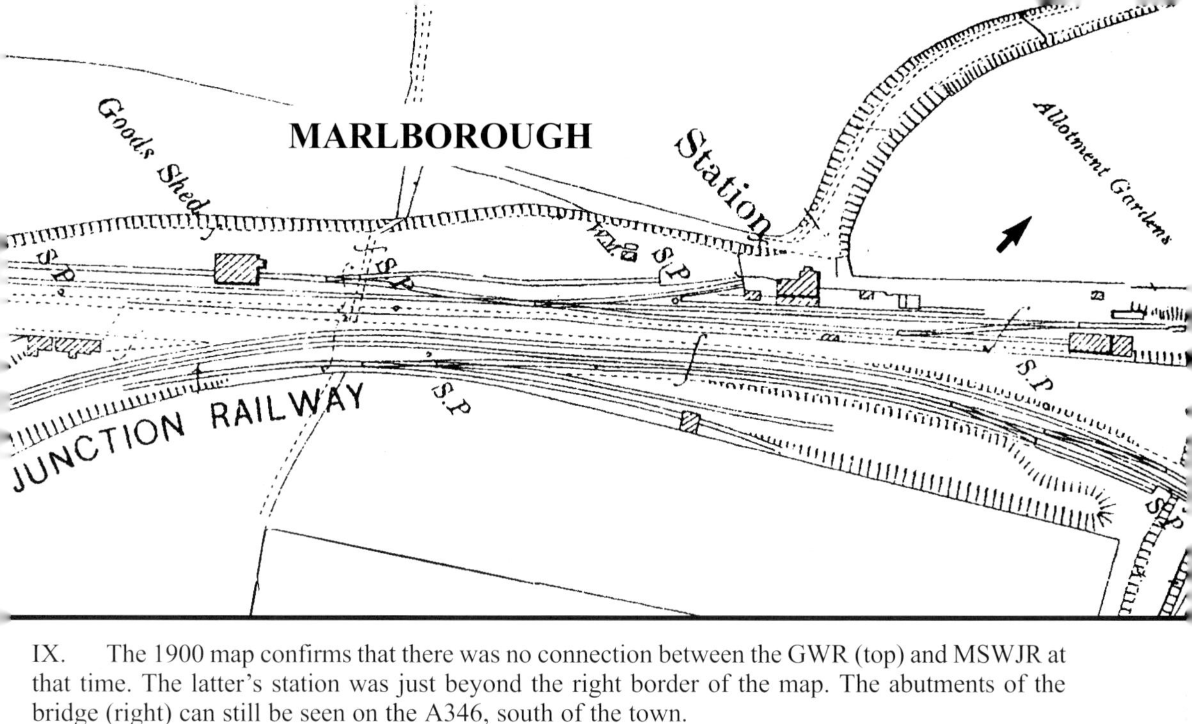

IX. The 1900 map confirms that there was no connection between the GWR (top) and MSWJR at that time. The latter's station was just beyond the right border of the map. The abutments of the bridge (right) can still be seen on the A346, south of the town.

56. A 1923 view reveals complete signalling arrangements. The MSWJR is to the right of the fence. There was a staff of 13 at this time and passenger figures were at their optimum. The use of a lattice post by the GWR was unusual. (NRM)

57. Two photographs from 23rd May 1929 feature "Metro" class no. 1499. By this time the maximum number of 14 men were employed. This included two guards, but there were also four loco crew and a shedman. The 15-lever signal box closed when passenger trains were transferred to the adjacent station on 6th May 1933. (H.C.Casserley)

58. The shed was built for broad gauge engines and later fitted with off-centre doors. The coal stage is under the water tank and the ash bin is to the right of the inspection pit. Official closure was in July 1933, but there is evidence of its use thereafter. (H.C.Casserley)

Marlborough	1903	1913	1923	1933
Passenger tickets issued	20571	38296	30595	668
Season tickets issued	*	*	27	-
Parcels forwarded	26402	28177	38992	4783
General goods forwarded (tons)	2968	2601	2089	*Included with Marlborough (Low Level) after 1932*
Coal and coke received (tons)	2115	820	2424	
Other minerals received (tons)	685	672	5076	
General goods received (tons)	4339	5261	5747	
Trucks of livestock handled	167	431	334	

(* not available. Seasons include holiday Runabouts.)

X. Gradient profile of the GWR branch. The MSWJR did not exceed 1 in 99 and its profile can be seen at the front of our *Cheltenham to Andover* album.

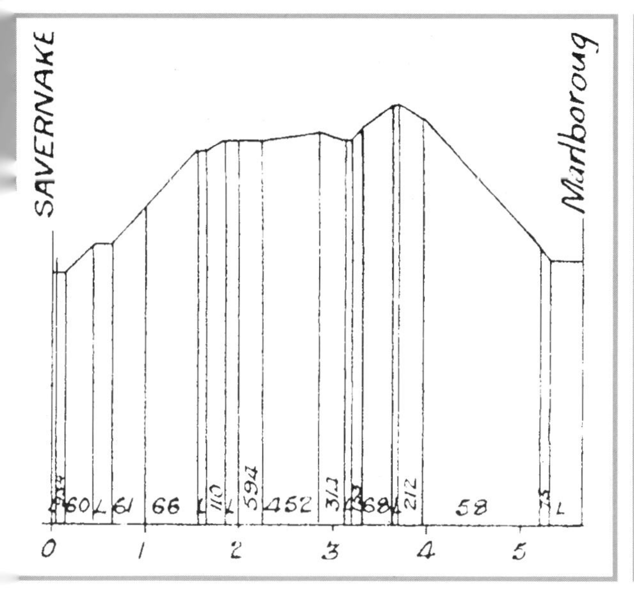

XI. The diagram shows the post-1933 arrangement with two single lines from Savernake (bottom) and a connection relaid to the original route to give access to the goods yard at the terminus. The passenger stations were "High Level" and "Low Level" from 1924 to 1933.

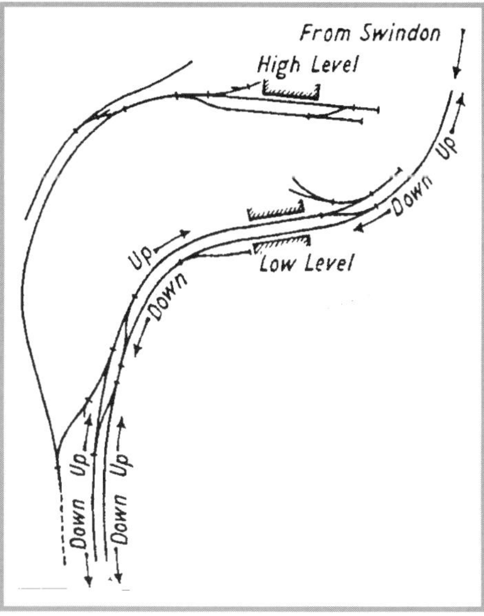

B
383472

59. The signal box on the right (apparently white due to its asbestos cladding) came into use on 6th May 1933 and was at the northern end of the two single lines. It also controlled access to this goods yard, the connection being behind the camera. (LGRP/NRM)

(lower left) 60. A grain loading rig appeared in the 1950s which received the harvest from tipper lorries on the platform and transferred it by means of a screw conveyor. The signals for the single lines are on the left. Only the one on the right was used after 1959. (Lens of Sutton)

61. A 1961 panorama includes a good crop of wheat in the six-foot and a working loading gauge. Goods traffic here ceased on 6th May 1964, but continued in the adjacent yard until 7th September following. Housing now occupies this site. (S.C.Nash)

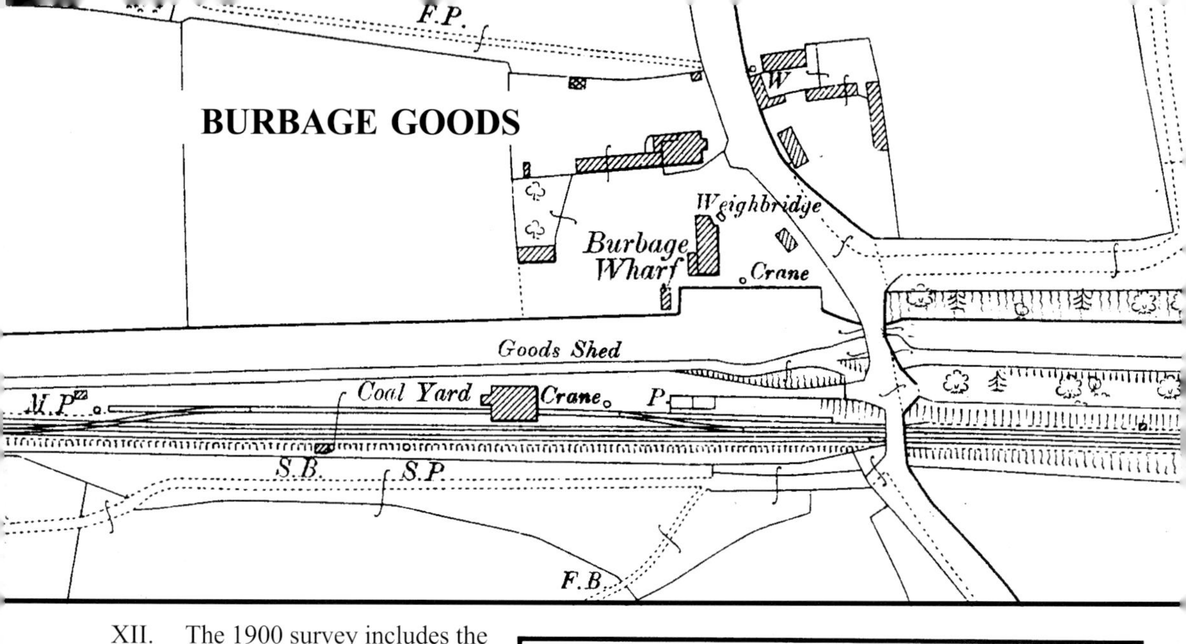

XII. The 1900 survey includes the two staggered road bridges, which were still a nuisance to drivers on the A346 over 100 years later. The siding originally provided the nearest place to consign goods for Marlborough. The crane could lift five tons.

Burbage Goods	1903	1913	1923	1933
General goods forwarded (tons)	1379	1104	1284	25
Coal and coke received (tons)	66	74	33	37
Other minerals received (tons)	68	10	828	799
General goods received (tons)	732	492	452	421
Trucks of livestock handled	121	139	336	44

62. The canal is not visible, but is to the right of the roadway in this 1927 picture. Freight traffic ceased to be handled here on 10th November 1947, but the signal box remained in use until 11th April 1948. (LGRP/NRM)

WOOTTON RIVERS HALT

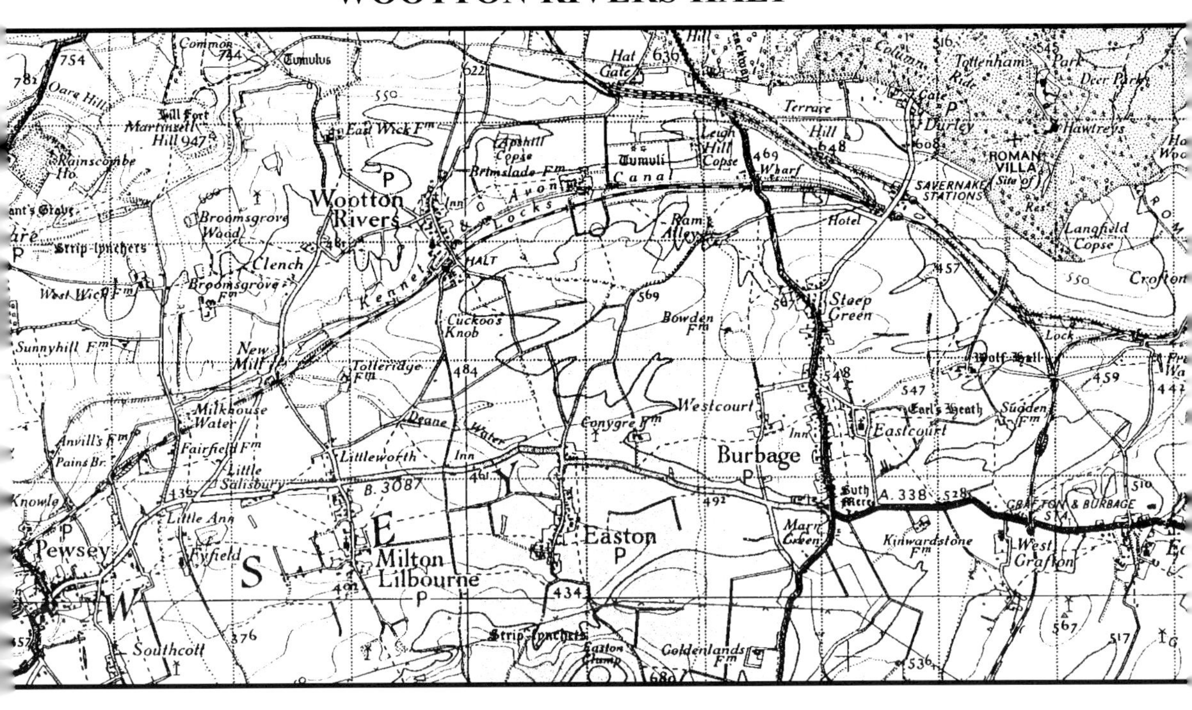

XIII. The 1947 revision indicates the position of the halt in relation to Savernake and Pewsey. The scale is 1 ins to 1 mile.

63. The halt opened on 24th September 1928 and was recorded from the east on a tinted postcard. The view dates from before 6th June 1934, as a signal box was opened that day, 50 yards beyond the end of the up platform. (Lens of Sutton)

64. The platforms were staggered for reasons of access. This and the next picture were taken on 24th February 1965 and both show pressurised oil lamps in the elevated position - unusual in daylight. (C.L.Caddy)

65. A "Western" Co-Co diesel passes the site of the six-lever signal box, which ceased to be used on 6th October 1963. It was used as a section break only at busy times and was closed from 1939 to 1949. The halt was no longer functional after 18th April 1966. (C.L.Caddy)

66. There was no trace of the structure when this class 122 railcar passed the site on 14th June 1974, while on a route learning trip from Reading to Westbury. (G.Gillham)

1A 62

B101

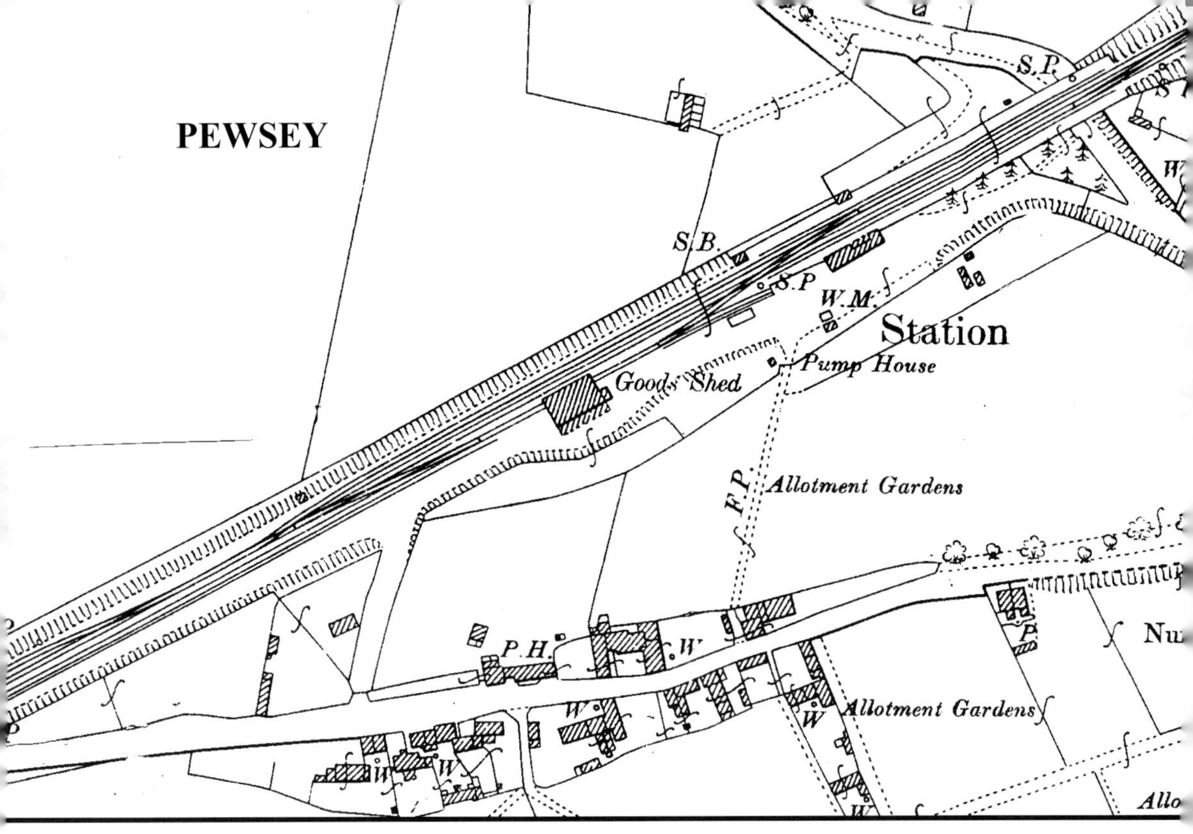

XIV. The 1900 edition must have been surveyed during the track doubling work in the previous year, as it shows some single line on the left. The upper track is an engineers siding. The other trackwork remained unchanged for about 65 years.

67. A postcard view from the early 20th century shows the standard Berks & Hants Extension building and the goods yard access from the up line, to avoid facing points. There were seven men employed in 1913, this increasing to ten by 1923. (Lens of Sutton)

68. This is the signalman's view in 1956. Note that the down starting signal had been repositioned to improve its visibility from a distance. The footbridge caused an obstruction as express train speeds increased. (R.C.Riley)

69. A "King" class 4-6-0 races through with the up "Cornish Riviera Limited" sometime in 1958, its smoke obscuring the signal box. The shelter near the locomotive was probably used for protecting mailbags awaiting up trains. A 30-cwt crane was located in the goods shed. (J.W.T.House/C.L.Caddy)

Pewsey	1903	1913	1923	1933
Passenger tickets issued	21345	20017	17447	10555
Season tickets issued	*	*	51	22
Parcels forwarded	38517	59313	65420	66925
General goods forwarded (tons)	4565	1865	3141	1019
Coal and coke received (tons)	778	971	593	1232
Other minerals received (tons)	1173	3040	2250	9802
General goods received (tons)	4638	3443	3320	3069
Trucks of livestock handled	584	155	115	41

(* not available. Seasons include holiday Runabouts.)

70. The signal box had 26 levers and was in use from 6th February 1923 until 2nd May 1966. Its predecessor was immediately to the right. (P.J.Kelley)

→

71. A second photograph from 1965 gives an excellent impression of the great expense that early railway builders made to impress all concerned. The local population was still only about 2500 in the early 1960s. From April 1966, the number of down trains dropped from five to two - one from Newbury and one from Paddington, arriving at 19.06 and 19.56 respectively. (P.J.Kelley)

72. Seen on 14th June 1974 is the reinstated morning down train, the 08.30 Paddington to Paignton. No. D1072 *Western Glory* is gaining momentum as it passes the site of the goods yard, which closed on 13th July 1964. (G.Gillham)

73. The 17.52 Paddington to Westbury slows for its penultimate stop on 7th July 1981. The footbridge and the up waiting shelter had both been replaced by that time. The first of the class 47s had been introduced in 1962. (G.Gillham)

→

74. The train of loaded four-wheeled stone hoppers bends on the change of gradient as no. 56050 passes the replacement up waiting shelter on 7th April 1990. (M.Turvey)

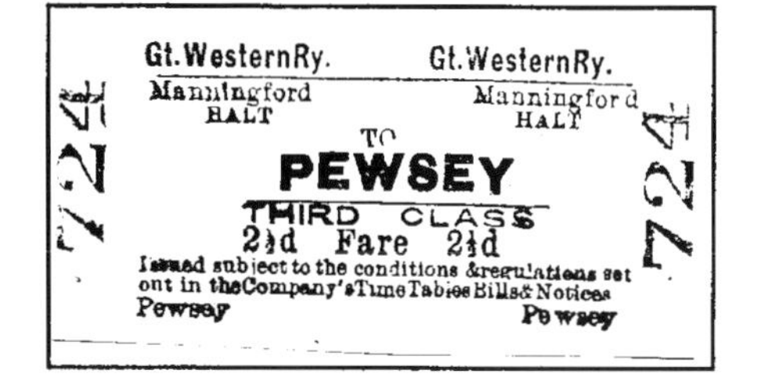

→

75. Railway architecture took a turn for the better in the 1980s. A new waiting room was built on the up side in the style of the original down side structure in 1984. Pewsey received the "ARPS & Ian Allan Best Restored Station" award in 1986. (M.J.Stretton)

050

MANNINGFORD HALT

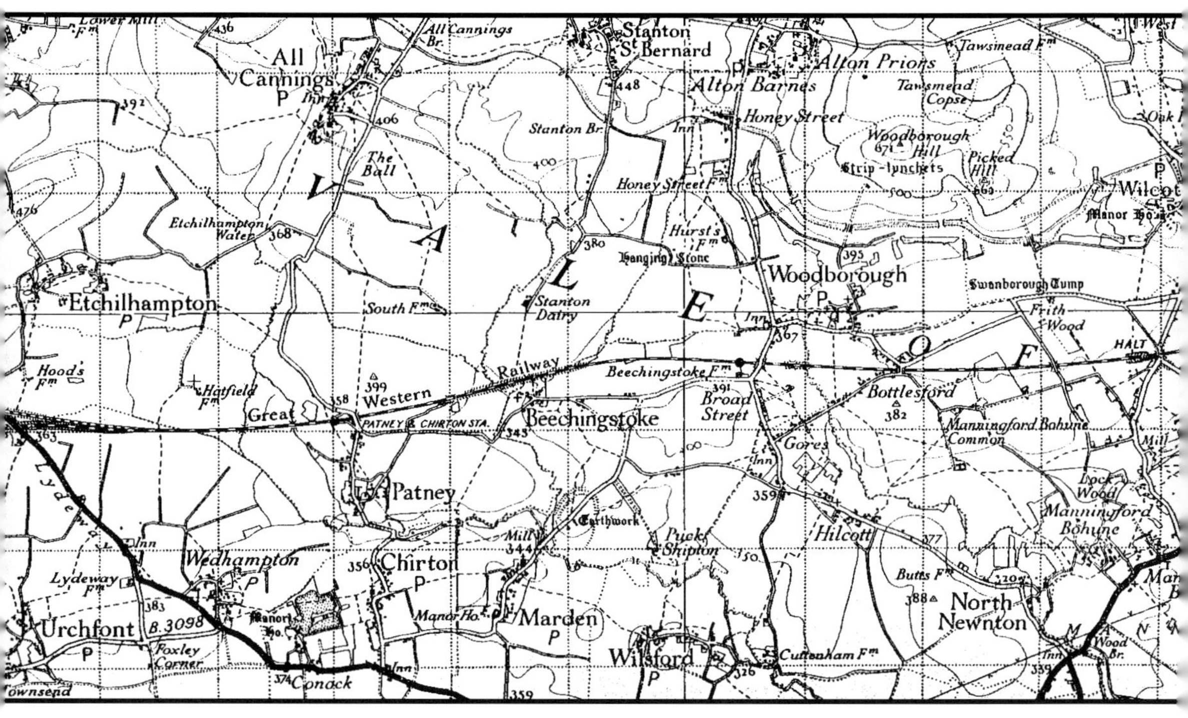

XV. The 1947 revision at 1 ins to 1 mile has the halt near the right border. It also shows the location of the two now-closed stations westwards.

76. These two photographs are from February 1965. The halt was in use from 20th June 1932 to 18th April 1966. This is a view westward. (C.L.Caddy)

77. Neither means of approach appear in this view towards Pewsey. There was a train about every two hours in each direction before closure. (C.L.Caddy)

XVI. The 1939 edition indicates that there was a footpath to the down platform and some steps on the up side.

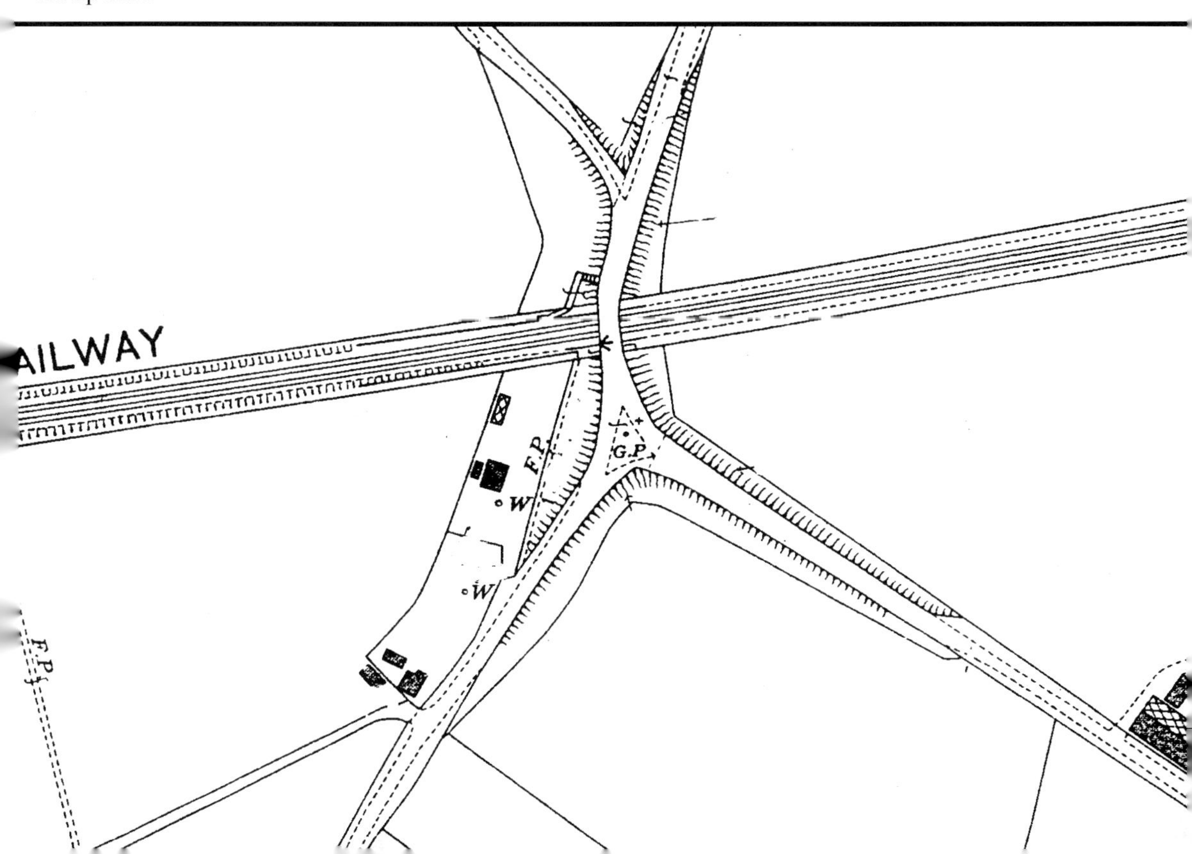

WOODBOROUGH

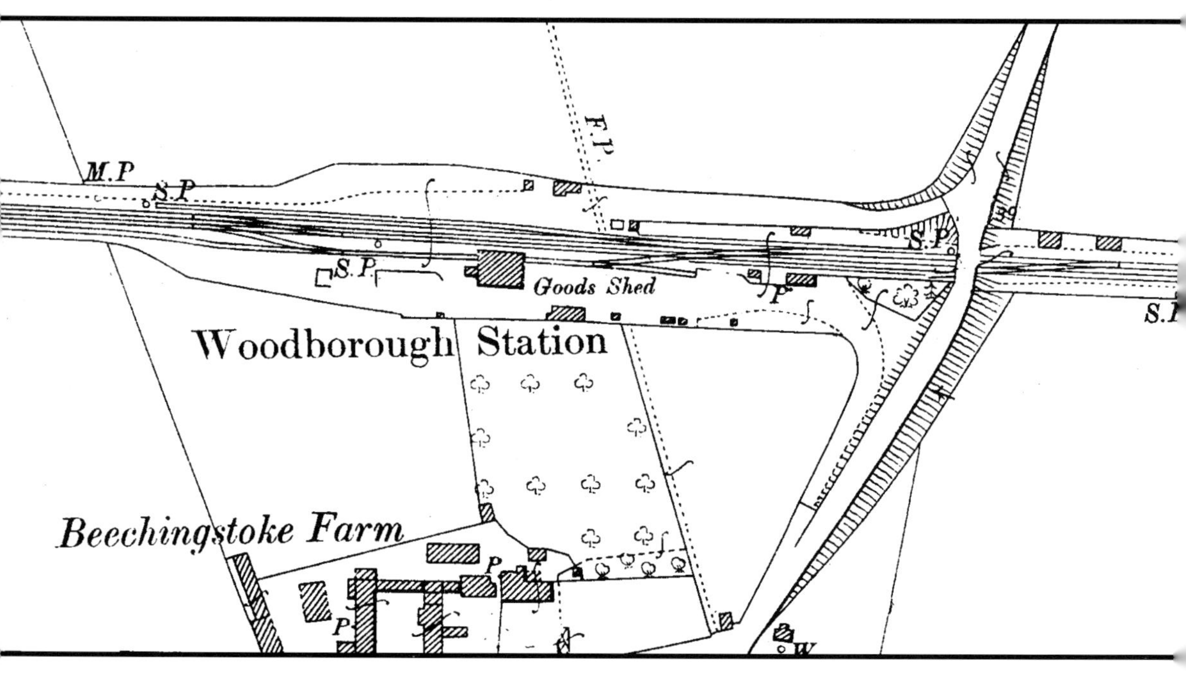

XVII. The 1900 map shows the layout at its optimum, apart from one extra siding that was laid on the south side of the site in 1903.

78. A reduced version of the standard design was employed, but still with the polychromatic brickwork. The haystacks are within GWR property and so were probably made from lineside growth and used by cartage horses. (K.Robertson coll.)

79. A staff of seven or eight was recorded in the 1903-38 period. The S and T boards indicated to travelling engineers if there was a fault with the signal or telegraph systems requiring their attention. (K.Robertson coll.)

80. Weather protection for passengers was minimal on this route, although the GWR was generous at other locations. The bridge carried an unclassified road which served a widely scattered and largely agricultural community. Passenger traffic ceased on 18th April 1966, the staff having been withdrawn a year earlier. (C.L.Caddy)

81. Another 1965 photograph and this includes the 1910 up refuge siding beyond the signal box. The former was extended to become a goods loop and the latter replaced an earlier model on 27th September 1944, and was in use until 22nd January 1979. The loop was extended further west in May 1979. Two parallel sidings were laid down in the 1970s for use by the engineers. These, together with the loops, were still in place in 2000. (C.L.Caddy)

82. No. 50035 *Ark Royal* works the 12.05 from Paignton in November 1978 and passes the site of the goods yard, which once had a 5-ton crane and closed on 15th August 1966. The down goods loop (left) dates from September 1944 and was extended towards the camera in April 1979. (G.Gillham)

Woodborough	1903	1913	1923	1933
Passenger tickets issued	16124	15037	10151	6694
Season tickets issued	*	*	36	28
Parcels forwarded	28456	43301	62905	116250
General goods forwarded (tons)	4772	4052	5712	1647
Coal and coke received (tons)	2892	1554	1059	960
Other minerals received (tons)	6650	8211	4174	5337
General goods received (tons)	4849	5395	4566	4334
Trucks of livestock handled	86	110	53	103

(* not available. Seasons include holiday Runabouts.)

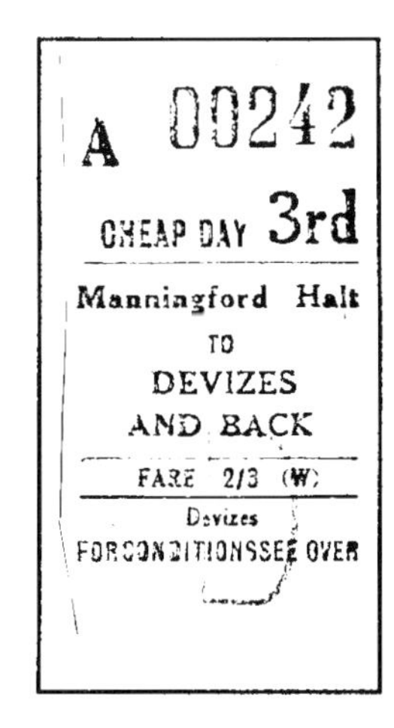

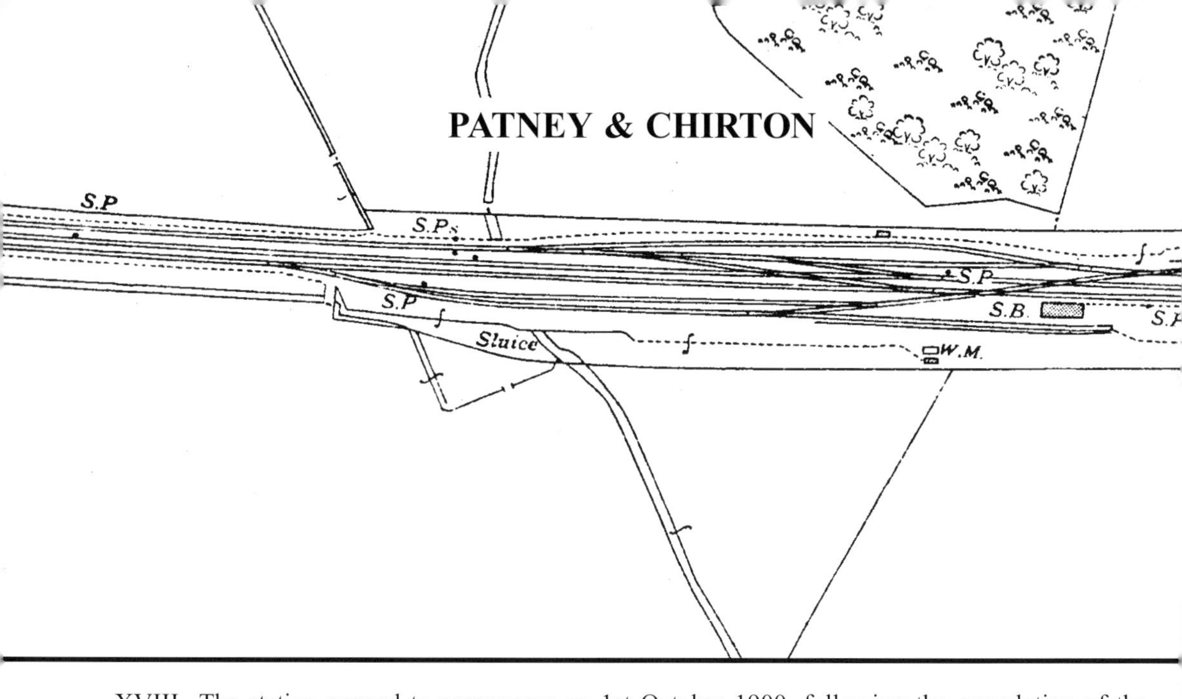

XVIII. The station opened to passengers on 1st October 1900, following the completion of the direct route to Westbury represented by the two lower tracks on the left. The upper one was for Devizes trains in both directions. The 1939 map shows the track at its optimum.

83. Being close to the northern flank of Salisbury Plain, the station handled military traffic associated with training exercises. A special long platform was added in July 1909 and is shown on the map adjacent to the top track on the right page. The signal box is in the background of this 1910 photograph. (Lens of Sutton)

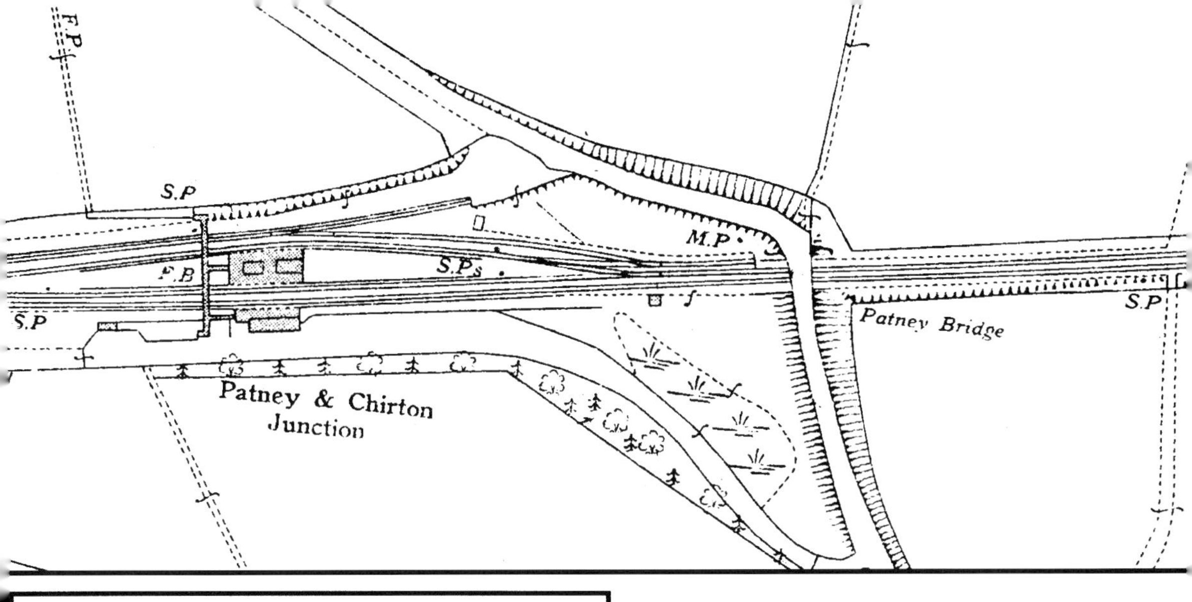

Patney & Chirton	1903	1913	1923	1933
Passenger tickets issued	10124	8127	7093	3650
Season tickets issued	*	*	9	14
Parcels forwarded	18761	32257	32721	3047
General goods forwarded (tons)	*Opened*	1629	1679	447
Coal and coke received (tons)	*for*	875	26	104
Other minerals received (tons)	*Goods Traffic*	3428	1759	447
General goods received (tons)	*1st October*	824	1144	850
Trucks of livestock handled	*1904*	37	23	58

(* not available. Seasons include holiday Runabouts.)

84. A 1921 panorama features the shielded entrances to the gents on both platforms. The two small villages used for the name would have generated few passengers - 27 a day in the best year - and not many would have changed trains here either. (LGRP/NRM)

85. Looking from the road bridge in about 1933, we see a lengthy goods train in the loop siding which branched off the military line. The end of the troop platform is on the right. Ten men were employed in the 1930s. (Mowat coll.)

86. There have been many instances of instability of the earthworks in the area. This photograph from May 1936 reveals that remedial work involved the bridge as well. (K.Robertson coll.)

87. Beyond the massive 70-lever signal box is the small goods yard, which was in use from 1st October 1904 until 19th May 1964. The train in the next picture is signalled for the track on the right. (A.J.Pike/F.Hornby)

88. Seen in July 1963, the branch platform was signalled for reversible running and the single line to Devizes was controlled by the electric key token system. Two trains from here on Saturdays-only terminated at Devizes at this time; one of them started here. (A.J.Pike/F.Hornby)

89. A 1965 record of the lavish provisions includes only two people. Staffing ceased in November of that year and the flower beds would be tended no more. The signs were already neglected. (C.L.Caddy)

90. Two photographs from 4th September 1965 include some activity, albeit non-stop trains. Trains for Westbury called only at 9.26, 13.26, 18.31, 20.42 and 21.00, the last one starting here. (C.L.Caddy)

91. No. D852 *Tenacious* of the "Warship" class speeds east over modern track on 4th September 1965. The old station would close to passengers on 18th April 1966, as would the Devizes branch. The goods yard followed on 19th May and the signal box on 6th July of the same year. (C.L.Caddy)

92. No. D1036 *Western Emperor* was photographed with the 06.35 Penzance to Paddington on 31st March 1975, by which time only the footbridge remained. This was because it carried a public footpath. (G.Gillham)

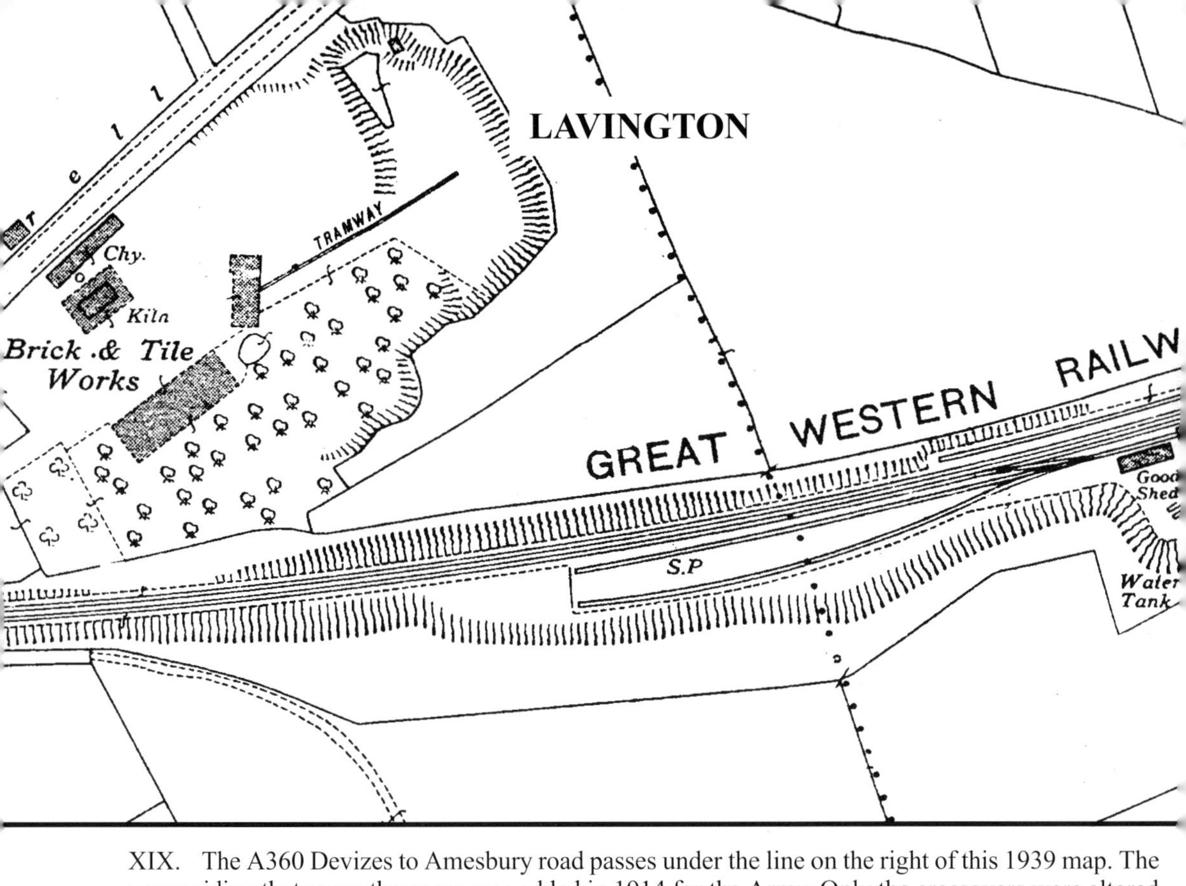

XIX. The A360 Devizes to Amesbury road passes under the line on the right of this 1939 map. The upper siding that spans the pages was added in 1914 for the Army. Only the crossovers were altered subsequently, apart from the extension west of the military siding to form a loop, which was in use from 1944 to 1964.

XX. The 1947 edition at 1 ins to 1 mile shows the relationship of this station and also the next one to the surrounding villages.

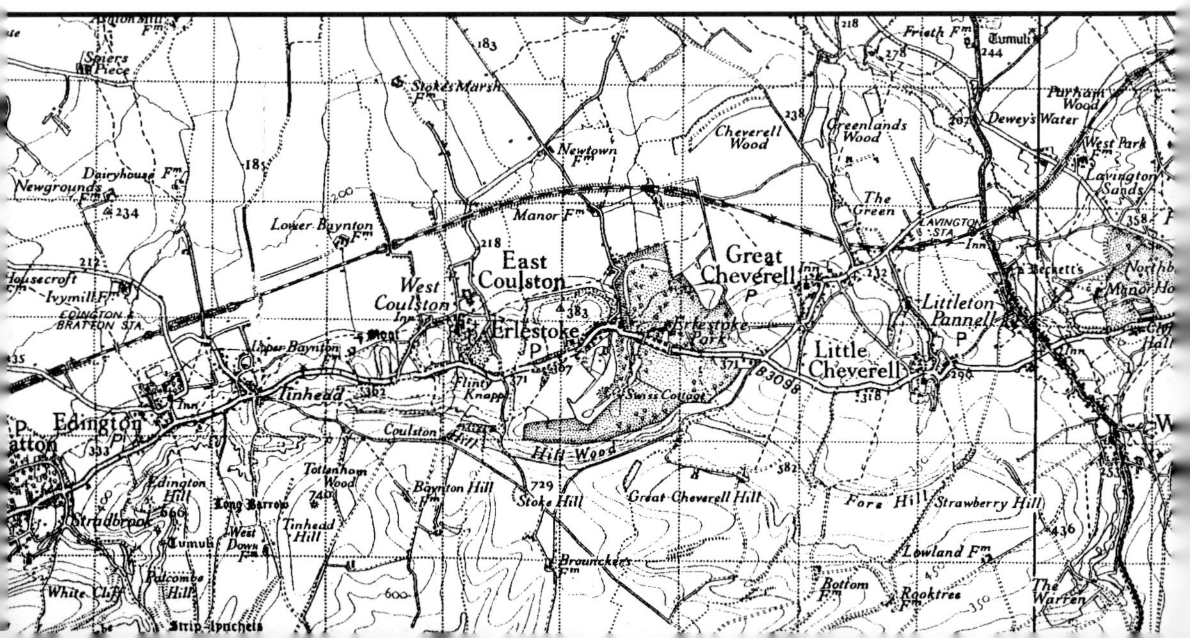

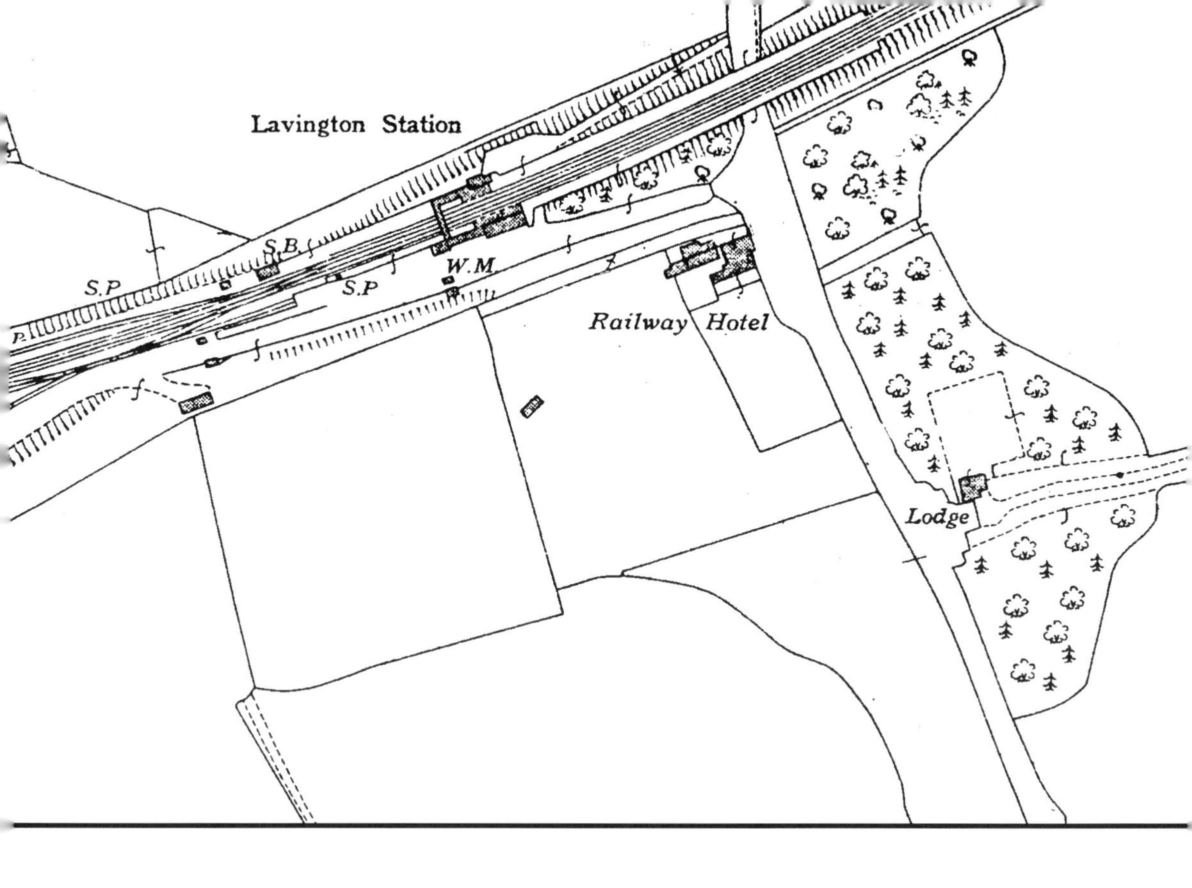

93. An early postcard features West Box, which opened with the station and the line in 1900. To the east was Crookwood Box, which was in use from 1934 until 1963, but only when traffic was heavy. (Lens of Sutton)

94. East Box and the post of a starting signal on the down platform can be seen. These existed only from about 1903 to 1914, after which both platforms were lengthened at that end. (Lens of Sutton)

95. The station was largely on embankment and to reduce the weight on it, the platforms were constructed of timber to a large extent. This 1921 westward view includes the up side approach road. (LGRP/NRM)

96. A down goods train is in the distance as an up passenger train loads. The nearest coach is a slip coach and has a vacuum cylinder on the roof, a guards ducket and a lavatory between the third class compartments. (Lens of Sutton)

97. A staff of 14 was provided in 1903, but this dropped to six, ten years later. Nine or ten was normal between the wars. Horizontal creases abound in this undated record. (K.Robertson coll.)

1A70
LAVINGTON

98. No. D7056 speeds through on 4th September 1965 and passes the goods yard, which closed on 3rd April 1967. A 30cwt crane was provided in the goods shed. (C.L.Caddy)

Gt. Western Ry. Gt. Western Ry.
Edingt'n&Bratt'n Edingt'n&Bratt'n
TO
PATNEY & CHIRTON
THIRD CLASS
1/4 Fare 1/4
Issued subject to the conditions & regulations set out in the Company's Time Tables Bills & Notices.
Patney&Chirton Patney&Chirton
1708 1708

100. No. D1012 *Western Firebrand* tears past the remains of the loading dock with the 09.30 Paddington to Penzance on 16th November 1974. The signal box, which had 22 levers, was used at peak times only and closed on 22nd January 1979. (G.Gillham)

99. Station staffing ended on 8th November 1965 and trains ceased to call after 18th April 1966. The final timetable showed only one down weekday train, the particularly useless 21.00 from Patney & Chirton. This photograph is from 1st May 1966. (C.L.Caddy)

EDINGTON & BRATTON

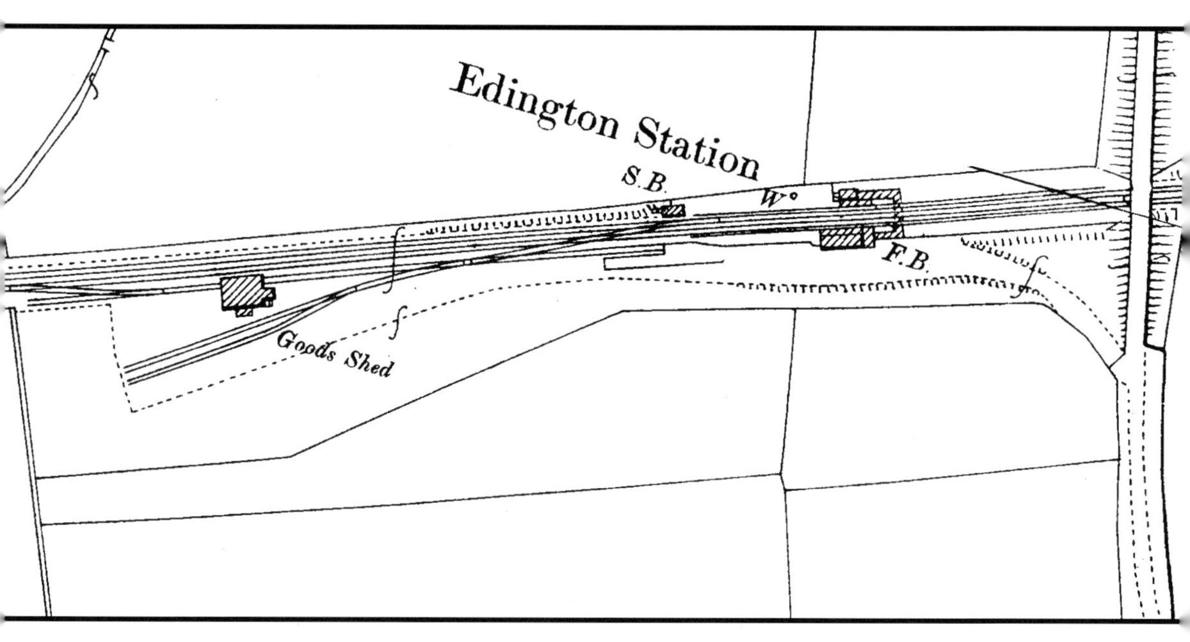

XXI. The 1901 edition reveals that a goods shed was provided, unlike the contemporary junction at Patney & Chirton. It had the usual hand crane rated at 30cwt.

101. A stationmaster plus four or five men were provided for most of the life of the station, which closed earlier than the others on the route, on 3rd November 1952. However, the goods shed was still extant in 2001. (Lens of Sutton)

102. The footbridge largely obscures the signal box, which closed on 22nd February 1959, and the goods yard, which lasted until 25th May 1963. The frame had 24 levers, but eight were unused. (LGRP/NRM)

103. The new route (known as the Stert & Westbury Railway) was engineered to the highest standard and had minimum curvature. The final timetable gave three down trains, weekdays only, one from Hungerford and two from Patney & Chirton. (Lens of Sutton)

Edington & Bratton	1903	1913	1923	1933
Passenger tickets issued	6765	6072	4511	930
Season tickets issued	*	*	-	-
Parcels forwarded	18928	28242	36797	5918
General goods forwarded (tons)	1125	837	904	110
Coal and coke received (tons)	1001	834	298	195
Other minerals received (tons)	1643	2739	1032	80
General goods received (tons)	1013	1377	1435	800
Trucks of livestock handled	17	28	38	26

(* not available. Seasons include holiday Runabouts.)

EAST OF WESTBURY

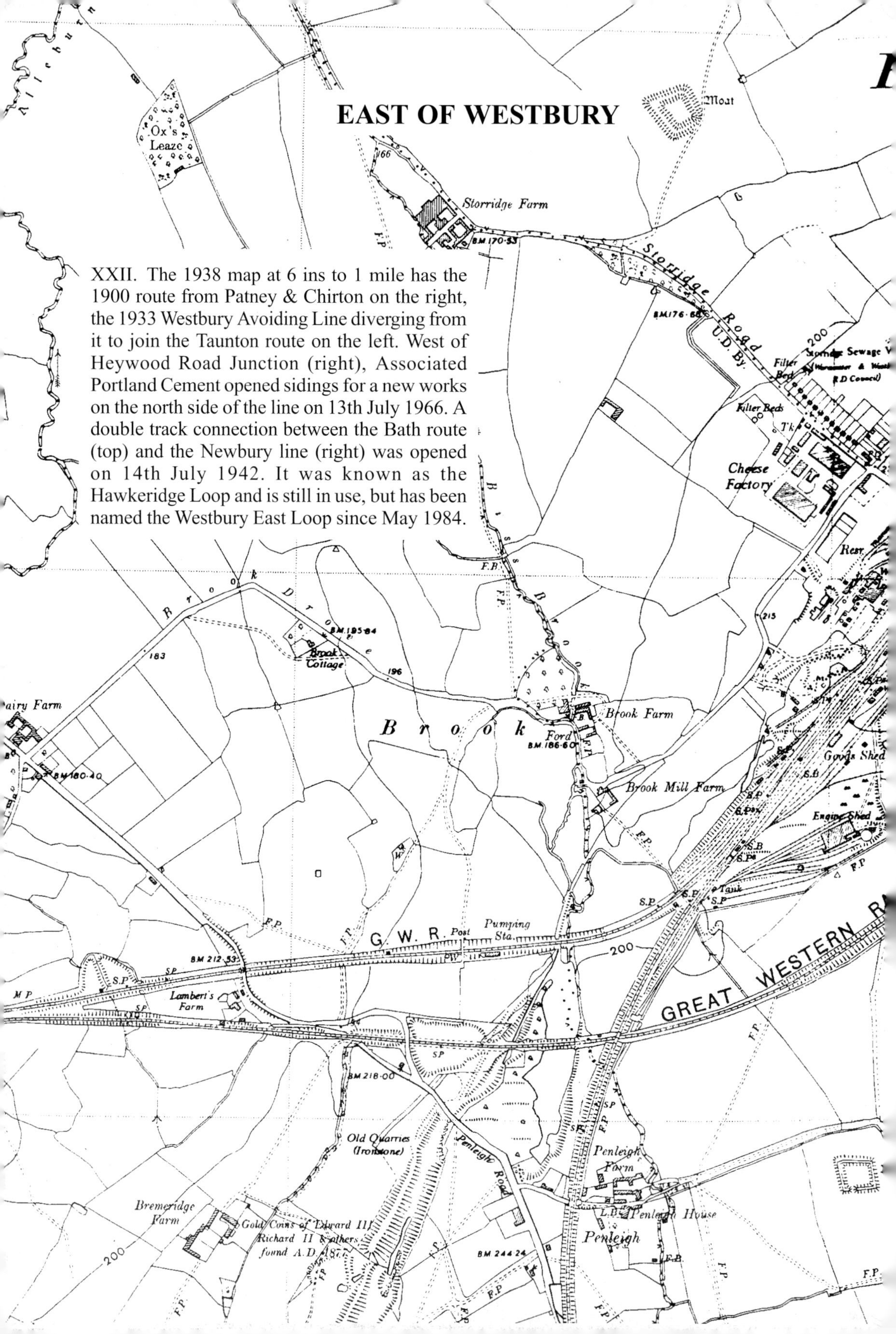

XXII. The 1938 map at 6 ins to 1 mile has the 1900 route from Patney & Chirton on the right, the 1933 Westbury Avoiding Line diverging from it to join the Taunton route on the left. West of Heywood Road Junction (right), Associated Portland Cement opened sidings for a new works on the north side of the line on 13th July 1966. A double track connection between the Bath route (top) and the Newbury line (right) was opened on 14th July 1942. It was known as the Hawkeridge Loop and is still in use, but has been named the Westbury East Loop since May 1984.

HEYWOOD
Shallow
Stone
Church Path
Glenroy
G.W.R.
Ham Cottages
Hackney Road
Sewage Works
(Westbury U.D. Council)
G.W.R.
-O-BRITISH SETTLEMENT
Westbury Lodge
U.D. By.
Heywood Road Junction
Holmedale
South Lodges
Frogmore Farm
Frogmore Road
Frogmore
Paint Works
Meadow Lane
Football Ground
Gas Works
(Westbury Gas Co.)
Coach Road
WESTBURY
Gibbs Close
Allot Gdns
Glove Factory
Drill Hall
Church
Club
Police Station
Meth Ch
Fontaineville Hospl
Pound Farm
Springs
Mill
Angel Mill
Baths
Prospect Square
Allot Gdns
Eden Vale
Eden Vale House
Indigo Factory (Disused)
Redland House
Lower Gooseland
Playing Field
School
Old Congl Church
WESTBURY
WESTB
Church
Hospital
Gooseland
Hill

104. Coal is in abundance as no. 33108 runs round its train in the reception sidings on 31st January 1990. Some class 33s were based at Westbury from January 1990 to March 1991. The fuel originated in the Midlands and was routed via Didcot. Ex-BR diesel shunter no. D9526 was in use by APC in 1965-70. Coal was still supplied by rail in 2001. (S.P.McMullin)

→

105. Heywood Road Junction is seen from a stationary slip coach, which had been shed from a down express. The 0-6-0PT will cross over, couple up and take the coach into Westbury station. The signal box was in use from 1st January 1933 until 14th May 1985. (H.C.Casserley)

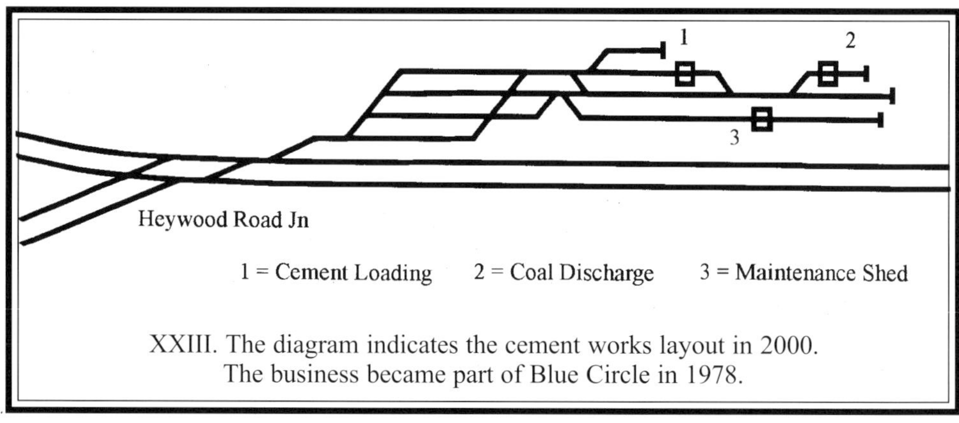

XXIII. The diagram indicates the cement works layout in 2000. The business became part of Blue Circle in 1978.

106. By the winter of 1981-82, only one locomotive-hauled working remained on the West of England main line, this being the 18.35 Paddington-Plymouth, with the stock returning on the following morning's 07.26 up service from Paignton. Under a cloudless blue sky, no. 50021 *Rodney* heads the latter train back on to the main line at Heywood Road Junction after the stop at Westbury on 23rd April 1982. The right post of the bracket signal controlled access to the Blue Circle Cement Works siding, while the motor-operated distant arm applied to the intermediate block signal installed when Edington & Bratton signalbox closed in 1959. (G.Gillham)

NORTH OF WESTBURY

107. The line from Bristol and Trowbridge is on the left as no. 73065 rounds the 1900 curve of the Patney & Chirton route with a Southern Counties Touring Society special on 13th November 1966. The train originated at Victoria and ran via Herne Hill, Redhill and Reading. It returned to Waterloo, passing through Exeter and Yeovil behind Bulleid Pacifics. (J.H.Bird)

108. Empty ARC roadstone wagons round the same curve on 8th May 1979, hauled by no. 47027. The adjacent track is known as Patney Siding; the one on the right was used for grain traffic for Nitrovit Ltd until September 1980. It was removed to make way for the new signal box. (T.Heavyside)

109. The distinctive chalet type architecture of Westbury Power signal box (opened 13th May 1984) shows up well in this evening view on 30th May 1989 as ex-works no. 56050 arrives with a lengthy train of empty Bardon and Yeoman hoppers forming the 16.02 Thorney Mill-Westbury down yard. On the left, no. 47526 waits while running round the stock of the recently arrived 17.45 from Paddngton. (G.Gillham)

110. The northern approach to the station was recorded on 19th August 1978 and the photograph includes the grain siding on the left, an almost complete array of signals and no. 50014 *Warspite* leaving with the 07.50 Paignton to Paddington. (S.P.Derek)

WESTBURY

←

111. The station kept some broad gauge trains until their demise in May 1892. Even when narrowed, the track was distinctive, as in the foreground. The inverted U section rails were supported on longitudinal timbers located by well-spaced transoms. (Lens of Sutton)

Other views and maps of this station can be found in *Salisbury to Westbury* and *Westbury to Bath*.

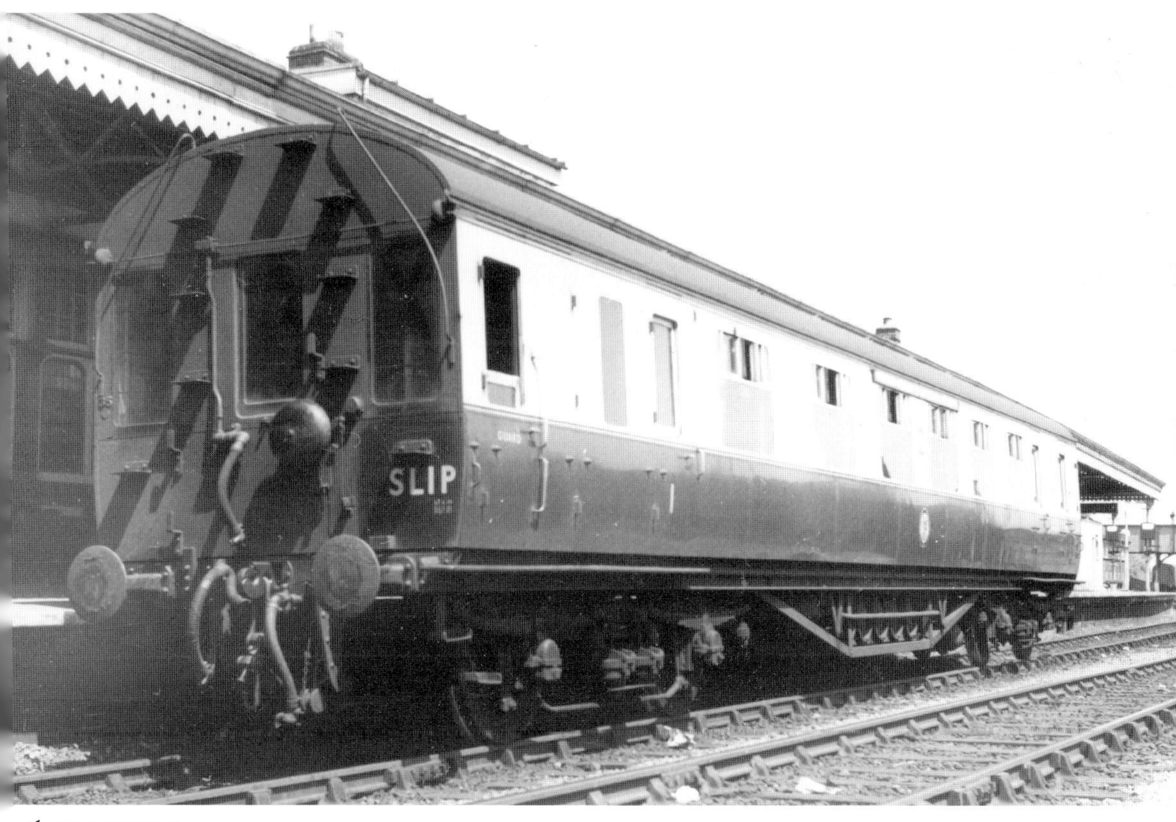

←

112. Included in this 1921 southward panorama is Westbury Iron Works, which had its own 2ft gauge railway system to the nearby quarries and also a private siding, in use from 1870 to 1941. The station had a staff of 130 in 1923. The number of platforms was doubled to four in 1899 prior to the opening of the route from Patney & Chirton. The western one (right) was usually used by up Salisbury trains.
(LGRP/NRM)

113. A slip coach of the type referred to in caption no. 105 is seen on 18th June 1958. At some stations, such as Savernake, the supplementary guard was able to uncouple the coach at speed and apply the brake to stop in the station. Note the gong provided as the "audible means of approach". Local goods traffic ceased on 1st November 1966.
(Wessex coll.)

114. The steam depot was opened in 1915 and its location south of the station is shown on the map. It is seen in 1961, with the water tank and coal stage on the right. Closure took place in September 1965. (R.S.Carpenter)

115. The diesel fuelling point at Westbury opened in April 1959, initially for the then-new diesel multiple units which were taking over many of the local workings in the area. However, over the years, main line locomotives became the principal visitors and on 6th October 1976 no. 46007 and no. D1053 *Western Patriarch* were among those waiting between duties. (G.Gillham)

116. The 15.15 Paignton to Paddington departs behind no. 50002 *Superb* on 6th May 1979. The signals are not set for its usual route, as it would run via Trowbridge due to Sunday engineering work. The signal box (left) has "North" painted out, as the work of South Box had been transferred to a panel in it on 6th September 1978. Middle Box had closed in 1968. Access to the platforms is via a subway from the building seen below the left signal. (T.Heavyside)

117. With the tall chimney of the Blue Circle Cement Works prominent on the horizon, no. 50025 *Invincible* hauls the Fridays-only 13.13 Paddington to Plymouth round the Westbury avoiding line on 23rd September 1983. The train is about to pass under the Westbury-Salisbury route. (G.Gillham)

118. From the 11th to 14th May 1984, the station was completely closed to allow a new track layout to be installed at the north end, controlled from the new power box. In this view from 18th May, no. 50012 *Benbow* waits with the 11.05 Paignton to Paddington "Torbay Express". The main alterations were the abolition of the former down Salisbury platform (left) and making the remaining three platform lines all reversible. (G.Gillham)

119. Colour light signals are evident as no. 47457 *Ben Line* heads the 09.55 from Paignton on 10th September 1987. In the centre background are sidings for locomotives and DMUs, but these were closed in March 1993. There are 17 sidings to the left of them for limestone traffic. (T.Heavyside)

120. Westbury became the centre for the despatch of stone from the Merehead and Whatley Quarries in the Mendips to destinations in the South of England. No. 59005 *Kenneth J.Painter* is returning empties through platform 1 on 16th August 1993. (J.Scrace)

Easebourne Lane, Midhurst, W Sussex. GU29 9AZ Tel: 01730 813169 Fax: 01730 812601

If books are not available from your local transport stockist, order direct with cheque, Visa or Mastercard, post free UK.

BRANCH LINES

Branch Line to Allhallows
Branch Line to Alton
Branch Lines around Ascot
Branch Line to Ashburton
Branch Lines around Bodmin
Branch Line to Bude
Branch Lines around Canterbury
Branch Lines around Chard & Yeovil
Branch Line to Cheddar
Branch Lines around Cromer
Branch Lines to East Grinstead
Branch Lines of East London
Branch Lines to Effingham Junction
Branch Lines around Exmouth
Branch Line to Fairford
Branch Lines around Gosport
Branch Line to Hawkhurst
Branch Lines to Horsham
Branch Lines around Huntingdon
Branch Line to Ilfracombe
Branch Line to Kingswear
Branch Lines to Launceston & Princetown
Branch Lines to Longmoor
Branch Line to Looe
Branch Line to Lyme Regis
Branch Lines around March
Branch Lines around Midhurst
Branch Line to Minehead
Branch Line to Moretonhampstead
Branch Lines to Newport
Branch Lines around North Woolwich
Branch Line to Padstow
Branch Lines around Plymouth
Branch Lines to Seaton and Sidmouth
Branch Line to Selsey
Branch Lines around Sheerness
Branch Line to Shrewsbury
Branch Line to Swanage *updated*
Branch Line to Tenterden
Branch Lines around Tiverton
Branch Lines to Torrington
Branch Lines to Tunbridge Wells
Branch Line to Upwell
Branch Lines of West London
Branch Lines around Weymouth
Branch Lines around Wimborne
Branch Lines around Wisbech

NARROW GAUGE

Branch Line to Lynton
Branch Lines around Portmadoc 1923-46
Branch Lines around Porthmadog 1954-94
Branch Line to Southwold
Douglas to Port Erin
Kent Narrow Gauge
Two-Foot Gauge Survivors
Romneyrail
Southern France Narrow Gauge
Vivarais Narrow Gauge

SOUTH COAST RAILWAYS

Ashford to Dover
Bournemouth to Weymouth
Brighton to Worthing
Eastbourne to Hastings
Hastings to Ashford
Portsmouth to Southampton
Ryde to Ventnor
Southampton to Bournemouth

SOUTHERN MAIN LINES

Basingstoke to Salisbury
Bromley South to Rochester
Crawley to Littlehampton
Dartford to Sittingbourne
East Croydon to Three Bridges
Epsom to Horsham
Exeter to Barnstaple
Exeter to Tavistock
Faversham to Dover
London Bridge to East Croydon
Orpington to Tonbridge
Tonbridge to Hastings
Salisbury to Yeovil
Swanley to Ashford
Tavistock to Plymouth
Three Bridges to Brighton
Victoria to Bromley South
Victoria to East Croydon
Waterloo to Windsor
Waterloo to Woking
Woking to Portsmouth
Woking to Southampton
Yeovil to Exeter

EASTERN MAIN LINES

Ely to Kings Lynn
Fenchurch Street to Barking
Ipswich to Saxmundham
Liverpool Street to Ilford

WESTERN MAIN LINES

Ealing to Slough
Exeter to Newton Abbot
Newton Abbot to Plymouth
Newbury to Westbury
Paddington to Ealing
Plymouth to St. Austell
Slough to Newbury

COUNTRY RAILWAY ROUTES

Andover to Southampton
Bath Green Park to Bristol
Bath to Evercreech Junction
Bournemouth to Evercreech Jn.
Cheltenham to Andover
Croydon to East Grinstead
Didcot to Winchester
East Kent Light Railway
Fareham to Salisbury
Frome to Bristol
Guildford to Redhill
Reading to Basingstoke
Reading to Guildford
Redhill to Ashford
Salisbury to Westbury
Stratford upon Avon to Cheltenham
Strood to Paddock Wood
Taunton to Barnstaple
Wenford Bridge to Fowey
Westbury to Bath
Woking to Alton
Yeovil to Dorchester

GREAT RAILWAY ERAS

Ashford from Steam to Eurostar
Clapham Junction 50 years of change
Festiniog in the Fifties
Festiniog in the Sixties
Isle of Wight Lines 50 years of change
Railways to Victory 1944-46
Return to Blaenau 1970-82
SECR Centenary album
Talyllyn 50 years of change
Yeovil 50 years of change

LONDON SUBURBAN RAILWAYS

Caterham and Tattenham Corner
Charing Cross to Dartford
Clapham Jn. to Beckenham Jn.
Crystal Palace (HL) & Catford Loop
East London Line
Finsbury Park to Alexandra Palace
Kingston and Hounslow Loops
Lewisham to Dartford
Lines around Wimbledon
London Bridge to Addiscombe
Mitcham Junction Lines
North London Line
South London Line
West Croydon to Epsom
West London Line
Willesden Junction to Richmond
Wimbledon to Beckenham
Wimbledon to Epsom

STEAMING THROUGH

Steaming through Cornwall
Steaming through the Isle of Wight
Steaming through Kent
Steaming through West Hants
Steaming through West Sussex

TRAMWAY CLASSICS

Aldgate & Stepney Tramways
Barnet & Finchley Tramways
Bath Tramways
Bournemouth & Poole Tramways
Brighton's Tramways
Bristol's Tramways
Burton & Ashby Tramways
Camberwell & W.Norwood Tramways
Clapham & Streatham Tramways
Croydon's Tramways
Dover's Tramways
East Ham & West Ham Tramways
Edgware and Willesden Tramways
Eltham & Woolwich Tramways
Embankment & Waterloo Tramways
Enfield & Wood Green Tramways
Exeter & Taunton Tramways
Greenwich & Dartford Tramways
Hammersmith & Hounslow Tramways
Hampstead & Highgate Tramways
Hastings Tramways
Holborn & Finsbury Tramways
Ilford & Barking Tramways
Kingston & Wimbledon Tramways
Lewisham & Catford Tramways
Liverpool Tramways 1. Eastern Routes
Liverpool Tramways 2. Southern Route
Liverpool Tramways 3. Northern Routes
Maidstone & Chatham Tramways
Margate to Ramsgate
North Kent Tramways
Norwich Tramways
Portsmouth's Tramways
Reading Tramways
Seaton & Eastbourne Tramways
Shepherds Bush & Uxbridge Tramw
Southampton Tramways
Southend-on-sea Tramways
Southwark & Deptford Tramways
Stamford Hill Tramways
Twickenham & Kingston Tramway
Victoria & Lambeth Tramways
Waltham Cross & Edmonton Tramw
Walthamstow & Leyton Tramways
Wandsworth & Battersea Tramway

TROLLEYBUS CLASSICS

Croydon Trolleybuses
Bournemouth Trolleybuses
Hastings Trolleybuses
Maidstone Trolleybuses
Reading Trolleybuses
Woolwich & Dartford Trolleybuses

WATERWAY ALBUMS

Kent and East Sussex Waterways
London to Portsmouth Waterway
Surrey Waterways
West Sussex Waterways

MILITARY BOOKS

Battle over Portsmouth
Battle over Sussex 1940
Bombers over Sussex 1943-45
Bognor at War
Military Defence of West Sussex
Military Signals from the South Coa
Secret Sussex Resistance
Surrey Home Guard

OTHER RAILWAY BOOKS

Index to all Middleton Press stati
Industrial Railways of the South-E
South Eastern & Chatham Railwa
London Chatham & Dover Railwa
War on the Line (SR 1939-45)

BIOGRAPHIES

Garraway Father & Son
Mitchell & company